T0307524

THE LITTLE HISTORY OF DEVON

THE LITTLE HISTORY OF DEVON

SUZE GARDNER

The History Press

For my friends
Linda, Di, Rich, Pam and Adrian.

First published 2021

The History Press
97 St George's Place, Cheltenham,
Gloucestershire, GL50 3QB
www.thehistorypress.co.uk

© Suze Gardner, 2021

The right of Suze Gardner to be identified as the Author of this work has been asserted in accordance with the Copyright, Designs and Patents Act 1988.

All rights reserved. No part of this book may be reprinted or reproduced or utilised in any form or by any electronic, mechanical or other means, now known or hereafter invented, including photocopying and recording, or in any information storage or retrieval system, without the permission in writing from the Publishers.

British Library Cataloguing in Publication Data.
A catalogue record for this book is available from the British Library.

ISBN 978 0 7509 9053 0

Typesetting and origination by Typo•glyphix
Printed and bound in Turkey by Imak

CONTENTS

ABOUT THE AUTHOR

Suze Gardner can't remember a time when she wasn't fascinated by history. She has written three previous books for The History Press. Suze has worked as a teacher and at the Women's History Library, London (Formerly the Fawcett Library). She has worked at Exeter's Medieval Underground Passages for several years, where she conducts guided tours and is involved in research. Suze also writes comedy plays with historical themes, which have been produced locally. She and her partner, Seal, live in a small village in mid-Devon surrounded by farmland.

ACKNOWLEDGEMENTS

My thanks are due to the staff of the Devon and Exeter Institution, Exeter Central Library, Devon Heritage Centre, Plymouth Central Library, My colleagues at Exeter's Underground Passages, Di the graphics whizz, Crediton Library, Councillor Stuart Penny and everyone who contacted me with interesting historical stories to share, lent me books and gave me ideas. As ever a big, big thank you to my partner, Seal, for having lots of patience and doing more than his fair share of the cooking.

INTRODUCTION

Devon's history is eventful to say the least. In spite of being a little isolated from most of the rest of the country, Devon has played its part in many important events from early history to the present time. Putting together *The Little History of Devon* definitely did not involve scratching around looking for things to write about! Rather, it was a case of choosing from the many important, interesting, entertaining and surprising historical events that have taken place in the county. Writing about them was a challenge in itself. This book is for people who are interested in history and want to know more without having to wade through hundreds and hundreds of pages. As a former history student the author knows how daunting that can be even to people who love the subject!

1

A LITTLE BIT OF GEOLOGY

Devon is the third largest English county and is made up of a variety of types of stone, some of which have been quarried for use as building materials, altering the landscape for thousands of years. Here are just a few of the more common ones that will feature in this *Little History of Devon*:

Granite – Dartmoor is famous for its extensive 300-million-year-old granite, formed by molten rock rising from deep underground. Visitors to the moor are fascinated by the weirdly shaped and weathered grey outcrops known as tors. These have given rise to a number of legends, but more of that later!

Limestone – Along parts of Devon's coast are huge pale yellow limestone cliffs around 400 million years old. These are made up of billions of compressed layers of dead prehistoric sea creatures and plants.

Red sandstones – The striking red sandstones of Devon were laid down as sediment between 280 and 200 million years ago and can most easily be seen on Devon's south-east coast. Perhaps its most famous location is 250-million-year-old Orcombe Point at Exmouth. Here the cliffs form the most westerly and oldest part of the Jurassic Coast.

Blame it on the USA

Only part of the Jurassic Coast is actually from the Jurassic era. Orcombe Point is Triassic and the most easterly part in Dorset is Cretaceous. The popularity of the *Jurassic Park* Hollywood movies is partly responsible for what amounts, in some parts of the coast, to an inaccuracy of around 150 million years!

Orcombe Point

2

KENTS CAVERN AND EARLY HUMANS

Kents Cavern at Torquay is a remarkable place to visit. The caves were formed around 370 million years ago from limestone that was eroded by water seepage. Curious stalactites hang from the caves' roofs, and stalagmites rise up from the floor. These have been formed over hundreds of thousands of years by dripping water that contains calcites and other minerals.

No one seems to know why the cavern is called 'Kents'. The county of Kent is over 180 miles away. An ancient story suggests that it was once believed that the cavern was connected to caves in the county of Kent and that they were used by the Devil to store evil souls. Another story suggests that Druids met there to perform sacrifices. Whatever lurid stories there are, it is a fact that Kents Cavern is very important in the understanding of early humans.

In the 1500s a man named Will Petre is said to have found his way into Kents Cavern. He picked up some odd bits of bone and flints that were actually ancient tools. Among the first and most important modern explorers of Kents Cavern was William Pengelly (1812–94). He was a geologist by trade with a fascination for archaeology. He made himself very unpopular with many Victorian people by rubbishing the idea that God created the earth in six days, ready made with all its different animals!

Kents Cavern would have been very different from the way it looks today. Pengelly and his assistants had to squeeze through tiny gaps and dig through layers of accumulated mud and stones. And all without modern lighting!

As Pengelly and later explorers dug through the mud layers of Kents Cavern and areas nearby, they discovered and began to excavate an incredible array of early man-made tools and, more importantly, human bones. These included evidence of Homo Erectus from around 350,000 years ago, Neanderthals who lived up to 40,000 years ago and Homo Sapiens – essentially the same as us. A jawbone from one individual that dates back over 30,000 years was found at Kents Cavern. Modern dating techniques suggest that this could be even earlier.

Early Devon people used Kents Cavern as a place of shelter but they were not alone. Cave bears also lived there in separate parts. The people were not in danger of being eaten though – the bears were vegetarians!

Other animal remains found at Kents Cavern include hyena, elk, horses, a species of lion, woolly rhinos and mammoths. Most of these are no longer found naturally in Britain and, in the case of mammoths and woolly rhinos, nowhere else either. Many of the bones in Kents Cavern were from animals killed and eaten by humans who lived there.

3

THE MID AND NEW STONE AGE 10,000 TO 2300 BC

Britain was once connected to Europe – and no, I don't mean as a member of the European Union! Until around 7,000 years ago south-eastern Britain was joined to what is now the Netherlands by a land mass known as Doggerland. Rising water levels due to the end of the last ice age and resultant storms covered Doggerland and separated Britain from the European continent.

Prehistoric people lived in various areas of Devon, but it is on Dartmoor where evidence of their presence is really plentiful. It is possible to see a number of different sites in a day and many can be seen after just a short walk.

High Dartmoor is around 1,400ft above sea level and the moor covers 25 square miles. Human habitation goes back 8,000 years, though this is scarce compared with later prehistoric eras when temperatures were warmer. As the climate warmed up, more people occupied the moors for its resources – stone and wood for building and animals for food.

> Dartmoor would have looked very different from how it does today as vast areas of it were covered in forests of oak, hazel and alder trees. Deforestation of Dartmoor began slowly.

Early Stone Age people were hunter-gatherers with nomadic lifestyles but by the mid-Stone Age people were changing to farming and a more settled way of surviving.

Flint stones worked into tools were left on Dartmoor by mid-Stone Age people. There is lots of evidence of this.

Dolmen

Tombs from this period are known as Dolmen. Dartmoor's best is Spinster's Rock in a field near Drewsteignton. Dolmen are usually made from three substantial granite slabs forming a triangle. These support an equally solid roof. Spinster's Rock top is 14ft by 10ft and originally would probably have been covered by earth.

A legend says that the three upright stones were once evil witches. They murdered a traveller and carried him to their hovel. Evil witches used body parts in their unholy spells. They were turned to stone by a good witch who just happened to be passing.

In the Stone Age, hunters were occasionally able to hunt and kill a small type of hippopotamus in east Devon.

4

THE BRONZE AGE 2300 BC TO 700 BC

At the risk of upsetting Devon cream tea enthusiasts, clotted cream may well first have been brought to the area by Phoenician traders around 3,000 years ago! They were probably the first foreign traders to reach Devon via Hartland point, which the Romans called the Promontory of Hercules when they finally got around to conquering Britain around 1,000 years later.

Migrants and traders from Europe came to Britain. They were known as the Beaker People because of the distinctive pottery they made. This was often a reddish colour with elaborate horizontal patterns. The beakers were used for cooking and storing foods. It may have been the Beaker People who introduced bronze-making to Britain.

Bronze was probably first made in the Middle East 5,000–6,000 years ago. The knowledge spread through Europe and then Britain that copper and tin smelted together produced bronze. The metal was harder than any other available in the Bronze Age. Weapons with much sharper cutting edges could be made using liquid bronze and moulds. Bronze was hard to break and it didn't rust. This Bronze Age technology was an important development in human history.

Today, Dartmoor can be very inhospitable, especially in the winter, but in the Bronze Age it was warmer. Much of high Dartmoor is little changed from this time. Bronze Age people began deforestation on a larger scale. People felled trees for building and began farming the cleared land. Trees once found in abundance on Dartmoor included oak, hazel and birch. Today these survive in small pockets, usually in rugged areas where felling trees was difficult.

Dartmoor granite made a very good building material for early settlers. As the stone weathers, softer parts dissolve to leave slabs that are useful as a building material.

In the Bronze Age there were more people living on Dartmoor than today. They led settled lives, grew crops such as barley and oats, and kept animals for food and clothing. Bronze Age people enclosed large fields with stone walls to keep their animals safe. Other settlements known as pounds usually had circular walls and covered large areas, often with houses inside.

Although Bronze Age people were farmers, hunting was still an important source of food. Flint tools were still made and used extensively. There is evidence that different groups on Dartmoor traded with each other, shared new ideas and possibly intermarried.

Round Houses

These were circular dwellings. The foundations and walls were made of blocks of granite. Round houses had low walls and high cone-shaped ceilings. The walls enclosed a space up to 30ft in diameter. Wooden roofs rested on top of the walls. Larger houses had a centre pole made from a tree that supported the roof, which was covered in deep layers of gorse or heather. The huts often had fireplaces and granite seats. Basic cooking pottery found by archaeologists often has patterns etched into it. People lived in communities with many huts. These were surrounded by a granite wall.

Men might have enjoyed relaxing in their huts after a day's work, but if an ancient story can be believed, women did not relax. Apparently, after cooking, cleaning and childcare all day, the women had to hold up candles made of fat so the men could eat in light. Women also got the less appetising meat and spent much of their time in the kitchen area separate from men, showing their lower status.

Grimspound

Grimspound is Dartmoor's most visited Bronze Age settlement. 'Pound' means 'enclosure'. Grimspound is around 3,000 years old. The site is easily accessible, and there is still a lot to see. The settlement is surrounded by a wall with a circumference of around 1,500ft and there were around twenty-four huts enclosed by it.

Stone Rows

Dartmoor still has over seventy Bronze Age stone rows. Some are very long and substantial, while others are shorter with smaller stones. Menhirs are larger stones placed at the end of a row. Some rows are single while others have many rows running alongside each other leading to burial mounds known as cairns. There is probably some religious significance in stone rows.

Upper Erme Stone row is the longest on Dartmoor and probably in the world! It runs for over 2 miles and has around 1,000 stones. Following Erme Row up an incline is like approaching a ragged row of misshapen monster's teeth. The experience is awesome and a little creepy.

Stone Circles

Some stone circles were used for religious rites. Some may well have been tribal meeting places.

Scorhill Stone Circle is arguably the most impressive on Dartmoor – one of its stones is over 8ft tall. The circle is 50ft in diameter. Today there are twenty-three upright stones with ten more lying down. Scorhill originally had around seventy stones. Unfortunately, the missing ones were probably removed in the recent past for use in building. Scorhill is dramatically beautiful, with its backdrop of stark moor. Legend said that animals won't go through the circle because they sense its fabled power. Sadly, the author has to report that this is untrue. On an extending lead, her friend's dog ran straight into the middle of the circle, relieved itself on one of the stones then sat down for a scratch!

The Legend of the Nine Maidens Stone Circle

Many years ago nine young women from Belstone on Dartmoor decided that they were bored with Sundays. Apart from attending church or sitting at home reading their Bibles, they were not allowed to do anything. One Sunday after church they sneaked off onto the moor and had a dance. This was strictly forbidden on the Sabbath!

Their punishment was to be turned to pillars of stone. They can still be seen on the moor today. Legend has it that sometimes visitors can still see the 'maidens' swaying as if to music.

Cists

These were a form of burial tomb. Essentially they were boxes with sides, top and bottom made from slabs of granite. Usually the bodies within had not been cremated. Sadly, Dartmoor's acidic soil and seeping rain means that there are few human remains left. There are hundreds of cists on the moor, though. Many have been opened. At Drizzlecombe on Dartmoor there is a good example of an opened cist. Visitors can peer into it, which is a spooky experience!

Round Barrows

Round barrows are burial chambers. The best site for these is Chapmans Barrows on Exmoor, where there are eleven together on a ridge; they are bowl shaped and covered in earth and turf. They vary in size from 10m in diameter to 25m. A spectacular site and a spectacular sight! The Longstone to the East of Chapmans Burrows is the tallest on Exmoor at almost 10ft.

In 1823 a young tourist visited Chapmans Barrows. He was alone because his friends were not interested in ancient sites. The young man forgot the time as he looked around the barrows and suddenly realised that the light was fading. It was a long walk over rough moor to his lodgings. As he hurried away he heard a screeching cackle. Looking back, he saw a giant flying reptile with enormous wings. The creature swooped and he threw himself into a dip in the ground under a bush. The animal flew away. For hours the young man didn't move. Then a search party found him. Later it was claimed he was a scientist trying to scare away artefact hunters. His Devon hosts knew him better – he was an accountant!

Wistman's Wood and the Druids

Wistman's Wood is on Dartmoor (some people say that the name is derived from the term 'Wise man's Wood'). It is a small ancient oak forest nestled in a hollow near the West Dart River. Druids – pagan religious leaders who worshipped nature – believed that Wistman's trees were sacred. The wood is certainly strange; its oak trees are stunted to only half their normal size with roots tangled among the granite boulders that cover the ground. Bizarre 'curtains' of lichen grow from the branches. Anyone who ventures into Wistman's Wood on a windy day and stays until dusk may find that the fronds of lichen begin to look like the swaying robes of the long-dead Druids. However, tales of witches making the trees walk about can be discounted!

Hollowed out rocks that look like basins can be seen on Dartmoor. Until quite recently some people believed that these 'basins' were made by Druids to mix up spell ingredients, or even to catch the blood of sacrifice victims! In reality, rain falling on softer spots wears the stone away.

Wistman's Wood, Dartmoor

At the end of the Bronze Age people began to move to lower areas because of worsening weather, which affected crops.

5

THE IRON AGE 700 BC TO AD 100

Dumnonii was the name of the Iron Age people who lived in the south-west, including Devon. The name means 'Deep Valley Dwellers' and is a Romanised version of an original name. Iron Age people in England possibly shared a similar language base with Europeans. The Iron Age was the last 'prehistoric' period. That is, the last period without native written records. This makes the Iron Age mysterious for many people who are keen on ancient history. (Written Roman records survive but were heavily biased and are incomplete anyway!)

Iron

The smelting of iron and production of iron tools and weapons led to far-reaching changes in society.

Early iron manufacturing took place in the centre of what is now Turkey. The knowledge spread through much of Europe, and iron smelting began in Britain around 2,800 years ago. To make iron, rocks containing iron ore had to be smelted in basic furnaces called 'bloomeries'. Ore-containing rocks were broken up and heated. This allowed the removal of bits of stone and other debris. The process of smelting was known as 'blooming'. The iron did not melt. Instead, small bits stuck together forming lumps or 'blooms'. As it cooled it went hard again and would have looked like a metal sponge.

To make iron tools, the iron was heated until it was red hot then beaten into the shape required. This is known as 'forging'. Early iron tools were probably luxury items available to the elite, but iron began to take over from bronze as a general material. This was because iron made far superior tools. It was much harder than bronze and more efficient than flint. Iron blades could be made sharper and stayed sharp for longer. Iron axes, blades for ploughs, nails, hammers and other tools were more efficient. Iron does have a disadvantage though – it rusts and decomposes over time. Sadly, a lot of Iron Age artefacts have not survived for this reason.

- Before smelting began, ancient Egyptians made jewellery from bits of iron meteorite that they called 'Black Copper'.

- Although we use the terms Stone Age, Bronze Age and Iron Age to denote different periods, it is difficult to separate them completely in terms of these materials. Flint tools were still in use throughout these periods for some jobs. Bronze was still being used in the Iron Age as iron was probably the preserve of the wealthy at first. Confusing? You bet!

Iron Age Trade with Europe

During the Iron Age, trading was common between Britain and Europe. Among goods traded were cattle hides, salt, grains and other foods, jewellery and gems, silver and gold.

Hunting dogs from Britain were popular with Europeans. The dogs were known for their intelligence, ferocious pursuit of prey, speed and stamina. Slaves were exported from Britain to Rome even before the Roman conquest. Possibly the people sent to Rome were criminals, or captives from different tribes.

Hill Forts

Iron Age hill forts are impressive historical monuments. Many of their earth ramparts can still clearly be seen today, usually on high ground dominating the surrounding area. Sadly, the wooden palisades (high wooden fences for extra defence) have not survived. There are around 2,000 hill forts in Britain and seventy are in Devon. Some are better preserved than others and some more easily accessible.

Victorian archaeologists gave the name 'hill fort' to Iron Age enclosures and sparked a debate that still goes on. Many of the largest hill forts on high ground with extensive earth banks and (probably) wooden walls were obviously defensive. They may have housed tribal chiefs and other important citizens, and were possibly administrative centres and a way to show off how powerful the leaders were. They would also have been a place of sanctuary for people from nearby communities in times of tribal war or natural disaster.

At other hill forts archaeologists have found evidence that suggests there were once Iron Age round houses inside. Wooden walls do not survive, of course, but fragments of pottery do. Smaller less well defended 'hill forts' were possibly animal enclosures or villages, and not forts at all!

Just to add to the debate about 'Iron Age' hill forts, many of the sites were first used in the Bronze Age (or even earlier) and some were later adapted and used by the Romans. Not everyone could have lived permanently in a hill fort – there wouldn't have been enough room!

An Assortment of Hill Forts

The remains of many of Devon's hill forts can still be seen. Some, of course, are larger and more spectacular than others, while some are better preserved and retain obvious features and others are more easily accessible.

Cadbury Castle near Bickleigh is reached after a steep walk. It is 800ft above sea level and, like most of its kind, has far-reaching views. During the English Civil War, Parliamentarian forces camped within its defences.

According to legend, an evil monster was killed by sling shots fired from Cadbury Castle after attacking people there. The monster's remains were apparently paraded around the local area to show the people how well they were being looked after.

Hembury hill fort is an example of early recycling! Some 240m up in the Blackdown Hills, the site was originally used by Stone Age people before an Iron Age fort was built. Later the Romans reoccupied it. Lots of earth ramparts can still be seen. Fragments of Stone Age pottery found at the site are known as Hembury Ware.

Clovelly Dykes is a large high hill fort near Hartland. It has over a mile of earth ramparts enclosing 20 acres of land. Parts of the interior were used for keeping animals, and trade probably went on from the site. The fort was also defensive.

Milber Down Hill fort near Newton Abbot is around 500ft above sea level. It had four rows of ramparts and is roughly rectangular in shape. Ornamental and household objects found there suggest a residential site.

Hillsborough Hill fort is over 300ft above sea level. The fort was defensive and overlooked what is now Ilfracombe Harbour. There were probably residential round houses and workshops there.

Denbury Hill fort, which is easy to get to, is located near a village of the same name. It is 159ft above sea level on a steep hill. There are still some high earth ramparts. The size of the hill fort suggests that it would have been used as a place of refuge and possibly housed a local chieftain and his warriors.

Iron Age Communication

Trackways, probably paved with wood, ran on low ground between hill forts and smaller communities allowing for easier travelling, better communication and trade. Ridgeways along the tops of hills could be used as lookout points or as an easier means of walking or moving goods by horse than steep-sided ground. Heavy wooden carts would have been rare, particularly in very hilly areas. Wicker chariots, while seen by many as war machines, were also used to transport goods. Wicker carts could be more easily repaired than wooden carts.

DRUIDS

In the Iron Age, Druids were the religious leaders in many parts of Britain. It was believed that they had magical powers and they were healers and teachers. Much of what we know about them comes from the Romans, who describe Druid sacrifices (sometimes human) and cannibalism! Of course, the Romans sought to discredit the Druids to supplant them with Roman beliefs and thus control the native population. A number of Devon place names are said to have Druidic origins. The word 'Nymet', which means 'sacred grove' (a Druid religious site), appears as a prefix to several modern Devon villages such as Nymet Rowland. There were (and are) many Druid festivals. These included Imbolc, which welcomed the end of winter; Beltane in May, which marked the start of the summer months; Lughnasa in August, a harvest festival; and Samhain, the arrival of winter in November.

Legend has it that Trojan military commander Brutus of Troy (Troy is now part of Turkey) visited Devon in 130 BC. The story says that before Brutus' arrival the people of Devon were being terrorised by a tribe of giants. Brutus and his army killed them all in a huge battle, allowing the locals to live without fear. Outside a shop in Totnes is a strange piece of granite that was, apparently, the first piece of Britain that Brutus stood on after leaving his boat. His intention was to colonise the island, but this didn't happen. Britain is certainly colder and wetter than Turkey. Perhaps the bad weather put him off!

The Brutus Stone, Totnes

The Iron Age in Britain continued into Roman occupation when new technologies were introduced. This is not to say that iron work has ever completely disappeared. Blacksmiths still work today, although it is becoming a comparatively rare trade.

6

THE ROMANS: CONQUERORS!

THEY CAME, THEY SAW, THEY WENT, THEY CAME, THEY SAW, THEY WENT

Britain's natural resources tempted Julius Caesar to Britain in 55 BC. But the invaders had to contend with the Britons, who put up more of a fight than expected. Caesar managed to land along the south-east coast, probably in Kent. He even established an outpost. Then things went wrong. The Romans became short of food and winter closed in properly. Caesar and co left.

In 54 BC he tried again. This time his forces managed to get inland. It looked like Caesar's invasion was going to be a winner; having an armoured elephant certainly helped! The Britons had never seen one and were terrified. Then the British winter set in again. Exit the Romans, who got nowhere near Devon – this time …

THEY CAME, THEY SAW, THEY CONQUERED

The name 'Devon' is probably derived from the word 'Dumnonii', the name of the Celtic people who populated the area up to the Saxon period. Dumnonii translates as 'deep valley dwellers' and was a Roman take on a previous unrecorded name.

Roman Exeter

In AD 43, ninety years after Caesar, the Romans reinvaded Britain more successfully. This was during the time of stammering, limping Emperor Claudius, known as 'the fool'. He was a more successful emperor than most people expected! In spite of his disabilities he actually came to Britain himself at this time. By AD 49 the Romans had reached an area they named Isca Dumnoniorum. The name Exeter is derived from 'Isca'. General Vespasian and the 2nd Augustan Legion built a large wooden fortress on high ground overlooking the River Exe. Isca became an important trading port and regional capital.

Isca Fort covered over 40 acres, and housed 5,000 soldiers and auxiliaries. At Isca the Romans constructed a wooden aqueduct to bring water to the fort, granaries, barracks, stabling and administration buildings. The fort produced bricks, tiles, metal objects and anything needed for the fortress to function. The most important building was the Bath House, built around AD 55. This magnificent stone and tile structure had room for a large number of soldiers. It had hot, warm and cold rooms and was highly decorated inside with elaborate mosaics and pillars. Just the place for the troops to relax away from the primitive surroundings outside the fort, and to warm up after the rigors of the British weather!

Isca Bath House was rediscovered in the early 1970s. This find changed the view of Roman historians as it proved that Exeter was a much bigger and more important fort than had previously been thought. Sadly, the remains of the fort are now buried again awaiting the day when money is available for a full excavation and partial rebuild. Let's hope it doesn't take another 2,000 years!

In the 1980s a stunning Roman mosaic floor that would have been part of a Roman house was excavated in Catherine Street, Exeter. Today it is in the town's Royal Albert Memorial Museum. Once seen, modern 'mosaic style' lino will fail to impress!

In 2006, excavations in the Princesshay area of Exeter revealed the locations of more Roman buildings, including a substantial villa that would have housed an important Roman official.

In 2016 the history and significance of the Romans in Devon changed again. To the delight of archaeologists and Roman history buffs, an important Roman supply complex was discovered in Exeter near the modern crematorium. Coincidently, the word 'cremate' is Latin in origin: 'cremo' means 'I burn [something] to ashes'.

In around AD 70 the 2nd Augustan Legion left Isca for the South Wales area. Isca Fort grew into a town with elaborate Roman villas, a forum, basilica (a building where important meetings and business took place) and other administrative and trade buildings. In AD 100 an earth bank was built around the town. This was replaced in AD 200 by a magnificent high wall built of purple volcanic rock, suggesting that local non-Romanised tribesmen were getting more troublesome. The wall was around 1⅓ miles long. About 70 per cent can still be seen today, although some of it has been altered over the years.

If you want to see parts of the original Roman wall in Exeter, look out for the neat bits where all the stone blocks have been cut to the same size with typical Roman skill and efficiency.

Exeter's Roman wall

The Romans were the first people in Britain to use cement, making buildings stable and longer lasting. This meant that some Romanised Britons began to accrue substantial property wealth and made them less likely to cause trouble for the Romans. Property wealth might be a good thing, but eventually it led to estate agents. Oh well, nothing's perfect!

In the 1940s a fragment of cooking pot was found in Exeter dating from around AD 300. So what, you might think – lots of ancient pots are found in cities and some of them are actually whole! Well, this particular fragment happens to be engraved with a Christian symbol known as the 'Chi Rho' and is the earliest evidence of the practice of Christianity in Devon.

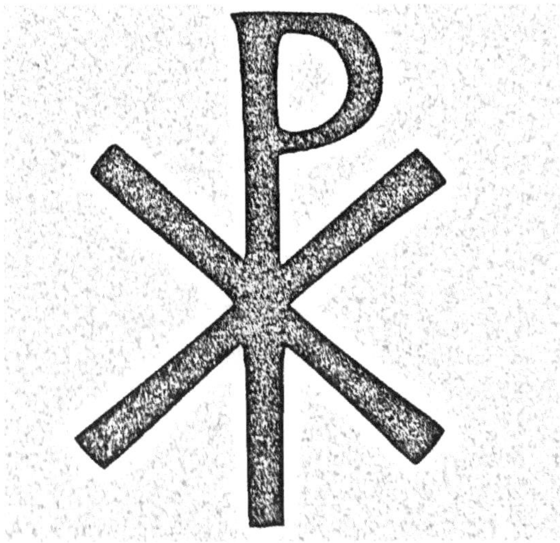

The Chi Rho symbol

ROMANS ROAMING DEVON

Although Exeter was their main base, the presence of the Romans in Devon is widespread.

The most important Roman road in Devon was the remarkable 180-mile Fosse Way. It linked Isca to Lincoln, Bath and Leicester. Axminster, a substantial fort, was located here near the road. Typical of the Romans' building skills, sections of the Fosse Way form parts of modern roads today. Devon's potholed roads are now often left for months before repairs are made. Given Roman efficiency, it's a fair bet that their roads were fixed much more quickly! At Kilmington there is evidence of a Roman road linking Exeter to Dorchester.

Topsham was an important supply port for Roman Devon. Any goods the Romans needed that were not available in Devon were brought in through Topsham. These included such Roman staples as olive oil, spices, Roman pottery gold, marble, silk as well as troops and administrators.

Another important commodity that was imported was wine, which was not produced in Britain – another grievance for the poor Roman soldier and all down to the blooming weather again! Roman exports from Devon included tin and other minerals, woollen goods, hardy British livestock, hunting dogs and slaves.

On the north Devon coast the Beacon fort was a signal station where Roman forces kept an eye on the troublesome south Welsh.

Villas

The presence of Roman villas, such as Holcombe, show that the many important Britons were Romanised to some extent. Most settlements, though, were still built in Iron Age style.

Hartland Point was once known as 'The Promontory of Hercules'. Hercules was a Roman and Greek god who, in the mythology of those regions, travelled the known world killing monsters and protecting the people. Over the centuries there has been a lot of speculation and argument as to whether he was a real person or not. If he was, then he apparently came to Britain and landed at Hartland.

Industry and Trade

Beer Quarry sadly contains no beer! It takes its name from the nearby village of Beer in south Devon. The quarry was first worked by the Romans over 2,000 years ago. They understood the useful attributes of this limestone, which has a pleasing creamy colour, is easy to cut without breaking, can be shaped into intricate designs and hardens on exposure to air, making it very hard-wearing. The Roman excavations with thick arches supporting the structure above can still be seen. Quarrying stopped in the 1920s and until that time was still carried out using many of the methods introduced by the Roman workers. Sadly, working conditions and safety hadn't improved since the Romans either!

Iron and tin smelting took place in Roman Devon. Most importantly, this would have produced weapons, but other tools, household items and jewellery would also have been made.

> Metal detectorists are not always popular with professional archaeologists or landowners. However, in 2014 a detectorist came up trumps by uncovering a hoard of over 20,000 Roman coins at Honeyditches, Seaton. The hoard is one of the biggest ever found and why it was buried in the first place is a complete mystery. The magnificent Seaton Hoard can be seen at Exeter's Royal Albert Memorial Museum.

Around AD 400 most of the Roman army left Britain, leaving a small army force and administrators. The Roman Empire in Europe was large and the numerous Germanic Saxon tribes under Roman rule were creating a lot of trouble, so extra forces were needed.

7

THE SAXONS: CHRISTIANITY

Saxons had lived and worked in Britain as labourers and auxiliary soldiers under Roman rule, and some settled in Devon. Then Saxon pirates began raiding Britain from the Wessex coast. By around AD 700 the Saxons under King Centwine had defeated the various tribes, including Devon's Dumnonii and their King Geraint – the last Dumnonii ruler.

That is not to say that all became peaceful. There were still skirmishes between Britons and Saxons in the 700s, culminating in Devon with Saxon King Athelstan expelling troublesome people of British origin from the walled city of Exeter as late as 928.

The Viking Threat Begins

From the 800s Viking invaders began to be a terrifying problem. For protection, fortified settlements, known as 'burhs', were built under the orders of King Alfred the Great. From the term 'burh' comes today's word 'borough'. In the late 880s Alfred began having silver coins minted and allowed Devon's four burh towns to mint coins, too. Burhs were heavily fortified settlements. It made sense to have the mints in burhs as it made it difficult for raiders to steal the newly made coins! Exeter was already sizeable when it was made a burh and is still by far the largest of Devon's former burh towns.

At the orders of King Alfred, Exeter's Roman walls were strengthened. Today, Lydford is a peaceful village popular with tourists, but in Saxon times it was also a burh and one of the most important places in Devon due to lucrative tin mining. Lydford was also a very wealthy trading settlement. Pilton is now a small part of the much larger town of Barnstaple. However, Pilton was also very important as a burh at the time of King Alfred. Pilton had substantial town walls for defence and security. Halwell is a rural village today, but was once a rich, powerful and well-defended burg and mint. By AD 1000 there were around forty-five mints in the country and King Alfred's coins were used as trade tokens in many areas of Europe as well as England.

Saxon Government

Remarkably, many Saxon government methods are still in use today! Shires were sections governed by a nobleman who answered to the king. They are more commonly known as counties today. Parishes grew with the creation of new churches, and today we have parish councils and larger county councils.

Open Field Farming

At Braunton Great Field, farming methods still run on the lines of an ancient open field or, more commonly, strip system. This did not mean that farm workers wore few clothes! Rather it was a fair share out of land. Though owned by a lord, tenants were allowed as many strips of land as they needed to support their families or as befitted their status in the community. Each tenant would be allocated a share of both good and less fertile land. The main problem with strip farming was that the paths between each strip were a waste of land. Also, competition often led to unfair shares! Eventually strip farming died out, except for Braunton Great Field and a few other sites. Some historians firmly believe that strip farming began in the Saxon era, some that it was early medieval. However, like many historical periods, they do tend to overlap in some aspects. Today the farm is run by dedicated specialists in their field, if you will pardon the pun!

Christianity

In Devon some people had adopted Christianity as a religion by AD 400, under the influence of missionaries from Ireland and Wales.

Church of the Holy Cross, Crediton

At first glance Crediton Parish Church seems very large for the size of town. Indeed, services are often sparsely attended. The church, though, is actually built on the foundations of a cathedral that operated from around 900 to 1050, when it was moved to the walled town of Exeter. From the early 1000s people were rightly worried about the dangers of marauding Vikings and wanted their cathedral protected. Crediton was still a very important Saxon town, which is illustrated by the fact that it had a cathedral in the first place!

Today there is still a Bishop of Crediton, although there is no cathedral in the town. Like the Bishop of Exeter, the Bishop of Crediton has an official home on Exeter's Cathedral Green.

Leofric was the first Bishop of Exeter from 1046 to 1072. He had to make do with a church rather than a larger cathedral. Often services had to be held outside to accommodate all the worshippers!

Bishop Leofric's Book

The famous 'Exeter Book' dates from 960 and is a rare and beautiful original collection of Anglo-Saxon poetry and riddles covering every aspect of life. And I mean every! A lot of the poems are quite rude and far too naughty for this book, which may be read by children! Curious? The Exeter book can be seen at Exeter Cathedral Library. It was donated to the cathedral by Bishop Leofric in 1072.

Two More Saxon Churches

Sadly, many Saxon churches in Devon and elsewhere do not survive today. Often they have been rebuilt at later dates, though sometimes there are a few Saxon features such as fonts to be seen. Here are two with a rewarding amount of Saxon bits: St Peter the Poor Fisherman at Stoke Bay nestles among trees and overlooks the bay itself. Pretty St Winifred's Church in Branscombe dates from the 990s. Rather than perch itself near the sea, St Winifred's is slightly more inland, probably to avoid Danish pagan raiders.

Saints and Missionaries

SAINT SIDWELLA

Sidwella from Exeter was an early Saxon Saint known from childhood to be kind, generous to the poor and a good Christian. Alas, she was unlucky enough to have an early version of the wicked stepmother who was jealous of Sidwella's popularity. Her father, Benna, a wealthy merchant, lavished love and attention on Sidwella, annoying her stepmum even more. Benna died suddenly, possibly poisoned by his evil spouse who wanted to get her hands on his money. Imagine her fury when she discovered that her hubby had left a lot of money to her, but the bulk of his estate to Sidwella, who he knew would use it to look after the rest of the family. Greedy stepmum then hatched a terrible plan. She bribed and possibly threatened one of her labourers into murdering Sidwella while she was praying at her favourite spot outside the town wall. Using his scythe, he quickly killed Sidwella by beheading her. As she fell to the ground a new spring of clear water sprang up at the exact spot. Sidwella was buried near the 'magic' spring, which soon became a place of pilgrimage, and the water became famous for healing the sick. The spring became known as St Sidwella's well. Several churches, each known as St Sidwell's, including the current one, have stood on the site of the poor girl's murder. Modern St Sidwell's replaces an earlier church that was destroyed during bombing in the Second World War. The spring disappeared many years ago. In Exeter Cathedral a

stained glass window shows Sidwella carrying a scythe. There are murals and other artworks depicting her around the city centre. No one knows what happened to the wicked stepmother but she must have been furious that most of her other stepchildren became priests and nuns and took their share of the family money into the church with them!

Saint Boniface

Missionary Saint Boniface was born into a wealthy Crediton family in 670. He wasn't given this name because he was handsome! 'Boniface' means 'beneficent', or 'charitable'. His birth name was actually Wynfrith. His Saxon father was a successful businessman and it was expected that Wynfrith would follow suit. This caused some argument as Winfrith had decided on a religious career and paid little attention to his business studies. Eventually his father gave up and allowed him to study and take holy orders at the monastery in Exeter. Wynfrith was ordained and became a religious teacher. He could have risen high in the church but decided that his true calling was as a missionary in pagan Germany. His success at gently gaining the trust of the wild pagans led the Pope to bestow the name Boniface on him. Boniface's most famous demonstration that Christianity was the true religion came when he cut down the sacred Donar Oak worshipped by a tribe near modern Hesse. Expecting the gods to punish them, the tribe fled. When nothing happened they converted to Christianity. Sadly, Boniface was murdered by pagan robbers at the age of 75. He was buried in Fulda Cathedral, Germany, and became the country's patron saint soon after. Today there are several statues of Saint Boniface in and around Crediton. Perhaps the most apt – carved from wood – can be seen in Crediton Church.

THE FATHER OF THE CHRISTMAS TREE?

After Boniface cut down the Donar Oak, a fir sapling grew in the same place. He adopted it as a Christian symbol and it was decorated to celebrate the birth of Christ. Eventually people began to put Christmas trees up at home. So, although Prince Albert, Queen Victoria's hubby, is credited with popularising Christmas trees in Britain, the idea goes back a lot further!

Copplestone is a quiet, ordinary village in mid-Devon. It takes its name from a Saxon granite cross, the 'Copelanstan' which once marked parish boundaries and is said to be the dead centre of Devon. Over 10ft high and elaborately carved, the cross is a striking sight, although its horizontal 'arms' have been missing since before living memory.

The cross is also rumoured to be cursed. This began when a travelling Saxon priest was murdered nearby. Anyone who moves the cross, so the story goes, will die soon after.

The Copplestone Cross

8

THE VIKINGS: RAIDERS

'Viking', which means 'raiding and exploring', is a term used to describe the Danish invaders of Briton. Today it is common to see the Vikings merely as murdering, pillaging savages but there was another motive for their attacks on England. They were also looking for good land to farm as this was in short supply in many parts of Scandinavia because of the cold weather and difficult terrain. Early Viking raids on England began in the late 700s in the north. Geographically this made sense as they were skilled seamen who merely had to hop across the North Sea!

VIKINGS IN DEVON

By the 830s the Vikings were trying to take Devon but with limited success. This continued on and off until 878, when King Alfred defeated them. The story of the Vikings in Devon is a long one. In around 850 they invaded the country near what is now Torbay but were defeated by the Saxons. There were numerous other attacks that were mostly repelled. Problem was, the Vikings didn't just run away, they burned every building in their path and stole anything of value. North Devon settlements, villages along the River Teign and near Exeter were destroyed.

In 851, Ceorl of Devon and his men had a victory against the Vikings at Wicganbeorg, probably in the lower regions of Dartmoor. In 878 the men of north Devon fared badly when nearly 1,000 were killed by Viking leader Hubba the Dane. Hubba was eventually killed in another north Devon battle near modern Appledore. Today the site of this battle is uncertain.

In 891 the Vikings invaded the Devonshire coast, killing many people. In 893 north Devon and Exeter were attacked by Viking raiders.

Ordgar, Earl of Devon, was a pious man. In around 961 he founded Tavistock Abbey, which became a very wealthy institution. Just the sort of place the Vikings relished. You guessed it – in 997 the Vikings attacked the abbey after sailing up the Tamar River. As with other raids, they stole everything of value including gold items and livestock belonging to the abbey. It is possible that the abbey lasted for over thirty-five years because they had been paying the Vikings off.

Lundy Island in the Bristol Channel is around 12 miles from the Devon coast. 'Lundy' is an ancient Norse word meaning 'puffin', indicating that Viking forces used the island. In the mid-1800s several ancient human skeletons were found on Lundy. Modern DNA testing has found that the remains are Danish in origin. Not unexpected, you might think, since the Danes once had a stronghold there. What is surprising though is that the skeletons were from people who were around 8ft tall!

DANEGELD

The English, including those of Devon eventually, had to bribe the Vikings not to invade again. This bribery became known as Danegeld. It was not a good idea as the Vikings soon realised that they could get even more goods and money if they actually came and took it, then asked for more Danegeld not to do it again! By the early 1000s Devon and many other parts of Britain were under serious attack from the Vikings.

The last two verses of this poem by Rudyard Kipling say it well:

Danegeld (1936)

It is wrong to put temptation in the path of any nation,
For fear they should succumb and go astray;
So when you are requested to pay up or be molested,
You will find it better policy to say:

We never pay *any*one Danegeld,
No matter how trifling the cost;
For the end of that game is oppression and shame,
And the nation that plays it is lost!

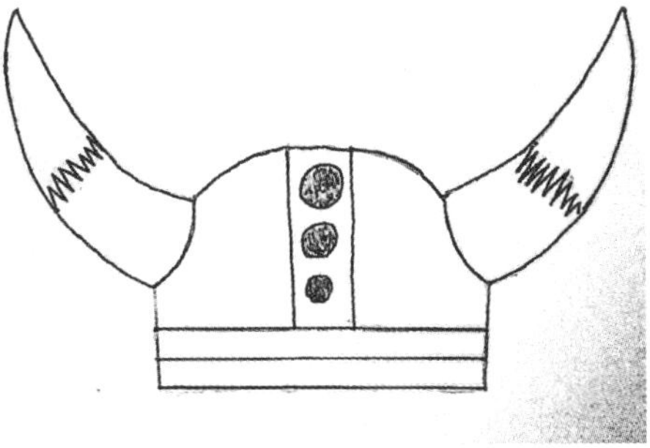

In 1001 Viking forces attempted to take Exeter after landing at Exmouth on the coast and decimating the fishing village there. Exeter, with its high defensive walls, managed to repel the Vikings. Instead they turned their attentions to the nearby village of Pinhoe, which was completely destroyed.

ETHELRED AND SWEYN

In 1002 Ethelred, King of the English, understandably became fed up with the pillaging Danes. The fact that some Danes were living happily amongst his people irked the King, who ordered them to be killed. Unfortunately, one of the Danes put to death in Exeter was the sister of Viking King Sweyn. Understandably he was a bit upset! Sweyn ordered his forces to attack Exeter by sailing along the English Channel and up the River Exe to Exeter. The element of surprise and the ferocity of the attack caught the people of Exeter off guard. Exeter was burned, killing many people. Everything of value was stolen

Later, Sweyn's son Canute would reign until 1035. He converted to Christianity and set about ordaining a number of English bishops. Canute may well have considered himself to be a Christian, but his behaviour wasn't! Like the times he lived in, he was quite violent.

Many people have heard the story of King Canute and the tide. Apparently Canute got fed up of people trying to butter him up to advance themselves. He decided to demonstrate that he couldn't rule everything and that God, in fact, did. Sitting on a chair on a beach, Canute ordered the tide not to come in, shouting 'Back, back I say!' Result – one wet king and a number of wet courtiers, who learned not to be so insincere!

One misty night in 1989 a man was walking his dog along Exeter's quay. Suddenly the air became noticeably colder and on the river the man heard strange splashing sounds. Peering into the gloom, he could soon make out a strange large shape on the water. Then out of the mist a curved boat appeared with lanterns burning at the mast. Fur-clad men rowed the boat and in the bows stood a huge fierce-looking red-haired man. He was shaking his shield in the direction of Exeter. The boat and its occupants suddenly disappeared. An elaborate hoax? The mind playing tricks? Or ghostly Vikings re-enacting their invasion of Exeter? You decide.

After 300 years of trouble from Viking raiders, English King Harold II finally defeated them in a huge battle in the north of England in 1066. Harold II was the last Anglo-Saxon king and his reign was to prove very short indeed.

9

THE MIDDLE AGES: THE CONQUEROR TO RICHARD III

KING HAROLD II FALLS FOUL OF WILLIAM

Harold II had been promised the throne of England by his childless brother-in-law, King Edward the Confessor. William of Normandy claimed that he had also been promised it. Harold was crowned in 1066 and William invaded. The two sides met near Hastings, where Harold was possibly shot in the eye. To add insult to injury, if you'll pardon the pun, William's knights hacked the dying Harold to bits – just to make sure. William took the throne. He was illegitimate and his father had died when William was still a child. This led to Norman noblemen jostling for positions of power, threatening William's position. He became vicious, paranoid and bad tempered – traits that continued into adulthood.

After taking England, William spent a long time quelling the English. In 1068 Exeter people refused to pay a joint levy of £18 imposed by William. Furious, he laid siege to the town. Gytha, Harold's aged Scandinavian mother who owned property in Exeter, was there at the time. She was understandably upset with William, especially as he refused to let her have Harold's body back. Exeter people rallied round her. Gytha was popular as she had endowed churches and hospitals in the town. Exeter officials met William outside the city to negotiate. He had one of them blinded and thrown over the wall. Gytha and the Exeter folk refused to give in. Eventually, William's men dug out the foundations of part of Exeter's wall and after eighteen days the people had to surrender. Surprisingly, William didn't have Gytha killed. Instead he banished her to Scandinavia.

- Gytha, it was said, had learned ancient witchcraft from her pagan grandmother. Superstitious William was terrified of her. He confiscated all her property, but he let her live. It seems that he was scared that Gytha's spirit might come back to haunt him. Gytha seemingly went back to Scandinavia. Did William ever worry that the old lady might curse him from afar? You can imagine the paranoid king wondering every time anything went wrong!

- Exeter men on the battlements made rude jokes about the French besiegers and even showed their bottoms. It has been claimed that this was the inspiration for the battlement scene in *Monty Python and the Holy Grail.*

William was worried that there could be more trouble from people in Exeter. In 1068 he built Rougemont castle on a hill of red stone with a good vantage point overlooking the city near what is now Northernhay Gardens. Only the gatehouse still remains today, but it is the oldest still standing in the country.

Rougemont Castle Gatehouse

Empress Matilda v King Stephen

The Norman period lasted for 300 years and there was a lot of rivalry for the throne from different factions. In 1135 King Henry I died, leaving his throne to his daughter, Matilda. Many people were outraged – a woman, it was thought, was not clever enough or brave enough to be a ruler! (Try telling that to Queen Elizabeth II). Enter Matilda's cousin, Stephen, who seized his chance and the throne after a lot of conflict. Some of the unrest was based in Devon and the rest of the south-west. Stephen was formally crowned in 1135, but his was an uneasy reign.

After Matilda was defeated, Devon's Baldwin de Redvers, a nobleman who had chosen the wrong side, had to make a sharp exit and lost all his lands, property and money. Undeterred, he took to piracy!

Heavitree Quarry

Heavitree Quarry on the outskirts of Exeter was begun in the late 1350s and was an important source of building stone for the town and others nearby. Heavitree stone is around 280 million years old and was laid down during flash flooding at a time when the area now known as Devon was arid and hot. The stone can be cut into large blocks, making it ideal for building, and it became one of the main materials used in Exeter and other Devon towns in the late Middle Ages. Unfortunately, Heavitree stone is susceptible to weathering and some buildings made from it were rendered with stucco in the eighteenth century. Thankfully, preservation techniques have improved since then and there are still many wonderful Heavitree stone structures to be seen. Heavitree quarry continued to operate until the nineteenth century.

No Lady!

A wealthy and handsome Ashburton man named Brietric caught the eye of a lady called Matilda but he wasn't interested. Then she married William the Conqueror and Brietric heaved a sigh of relief. But Matilda would have her revenge for Brietric's rejection – William had Brietric slung into prison, where he died because of the terrible conditions.

The Building Bishop

In 1107 William Warelwast became Exeter's third bishop. He was a nephew of William the Conqueror and came from Normandy. From 1114 to 1133 Bishop Warelwast built Exeter's first cathedral, replacing the old Saxon structure. Well, he built some of it. The whole thing wasn't finished until the early 1200s! A building the size and height of a cathedral was a major undertaking. The two huge square towers on either side of the cathedral are the most significant Norman parts left.

Most of the cathedral didn't last long though! A building style known as Decorated Gothic became popular and major rebuilding began again. An easily recognised Decorated Gothic feature is the flying buttress – stone pillars built against the cathedral walls at right angles to take some of the weight. A more artistic feature is the taller pointed windows with elaborately carved vertical stone tracers. This rebuild was completed around 1400 and can still be seen today.

Exeter Cathedral has the longest continuous medieval vaulted ceiling in the world at 315ft. At one time if you went to see it you would get a stiff neck as you stood in amazement looking up! Nowadays it's easier. The cathedral's resourceful and helpful staff have cleverly positioned a mirror facing upwards a few feet from the floor. Through this it is possible to see the entire ceiling in all its glory.

Exeter is among the few places to have a mayor executed. In 1283 John Pycot became Dean of the Cathedral. He was a friend of the bishop. Pycot was unpopular. The cathedral staff protested, especially Walter Lechlade, who had been treated badly by Pycot. In November 1283, Lechlade was murdered, probably by Pycot's supporters. Pycot and the Lord Mayor Alured de Porta, who seemingly knew about the murder, were tried along with the murderers. The case went on for two years. Then, at Christmas 1285, an annoyed King Edward I had to go to Exeter to sit in judgement. He sentenced five people to hang including the Mayor! Sneaky Pycot survived by claiming 'benefit of clergy', a way for churchmen to avoid punishment in civic courts as the church had its own system.

Abbeys and Priories

In Devon many religious houses were established in the medieval period and some can still be seen. From functioning religious establishments to picturesque ruins, Devon has lots!

St Nicholas Priory was founded in Exeter in 1087. It became a Benedictine monastery and was very wealthy, owning lots of land. Medieval parts still to be seen include the wonderful arched cellar.

Buckfast Abbey was built in the 1130s and is still a working abbey. It is well known for its honey production and even more famous for the fortified wine it has been making since the 1880s. Buckfast wine is still sold in many areas of the country today.

Buckland Abbey was founded in the 1270s. For centuries it has been a grand house although the conversion kept a lot of original abbey features that can still be seen.

Cowick Priory, founded in the 1100s, became a house in the 1540s. In 1963 it became the Cowick Barton Inn – an atmospheric pub that is supposedly haunted! Among the ghosts is that of a little Victorian boy who was sick and lived in an attic room, who can apparently still be seen peering out.

Polsloe Priory (St Katherine's) was founded in the 1150s. It was a nunnery, one of the first in Devon, with the nuns the daughters of wealthy Devon families. Part of the original priory building still remains.

Frithelstock Priory has been a ruin for over 400 years but still influences modern language. The term 'club,' meaning people with a shared interest, began at Frithelstock. When monks travelled they went in pairs to keep an eye on each other to ensure that neither looked at women nor did even naughtier things. To discourage this each monk had a heavy club to give a misbehaving colleague a hefty whack. Quite what they would make of amorous night 'club' goers today can only be imagined!

Frithelstock Priory ruins

MEDIEVAL CHURCHES IN DEVON

Sadly, many medieval churches in Devon were rebuilt or altered significantly at later dates, although there are still some with medieval features. As well as the towers of Exeter's cathedral, the arches of St Peter's' Church in Crediton are partly medieval. Here are a few more Devon churches with medieval bits that are easy to see:

All Saints Church, Clovelly, has some lovely barrel vaulting; St Olave's Church, Exeter, was Gytha's own chapel and still has a tower built in her time; St Mary's Church, Kentisbeare, was consecrated in the 1250s and still has a wonderful carved screen; St Cyres, St Cuy and St Julitta Church, Newton St Cyres, has a tower from the 1200s and barrel vaulting from the 1300s; St Pancras Church, Exeter, is very atmospheric in spite of being almost surrounded by modern shops. Parts date from the 1190s. It is a sanctuary for harassed shoppers and is the author's favourite Devon church!

In 1335 John Grandisson built St Mary's Church in Ottery St Mary. It had a very loud bell to ward off evil pixies. In those superstitious days people believed that pixies were to blame for cattle falling sick, accidents, things going missing, evil spells and a host of other misfortunes. On the day the church bell was delivered the cart went in the wrong direction. The pixies' doing! The vicar began to pray loudly. The cart turned back to the church. Less educated parishioners put this down to the pixies being frightened off by the religious words!

St Lawrence's Church stood on Exeter High Street on the site of the modern Co-op Bank from the 1200s until 4 May 1942. Sadly, the church was destroyed during Exeter's worst bombing raid and the organist who bravely continued to play *Jerusalem* was killed. All that remains today is a plaque commemorating its destruction. Or is that really all? People claim to have heard the ghostly tune on the anniversary of the tragic event.

Danes Castle

The demolition of an old reservoir in 1992 proved exciting for Exeter's archaeologists as they uncovered the remains of Danes Castle dating from 1136. King Stephen built the castle to threaten and subdue Exeter residents who, with the support of the powerful 1st Earl of Devon Baldwin de Redvers, backed his cousin Queen Matilda's claim to the throne. She actually had every right to it as her dead father had been King Henry I. Alas, for women's rights! In those days most people believed that women were not strong or determined enough to rule, especially as they spent so much time having babies. In fact, one of her children became King Henry II after King Stephen and his son, Eustace, died.

ATTONEMENT

Sir William de Tracey, Baron of Bradninch and Moretonhampstead, was born in Devon in 1133. He was kind to the poor, built sanctuaries for lepers and orphanages, helped the elderly and founded several churches. A nice man you might think. Well, he hadn't always been. In 1170, William was one of the knights who murdered Archbishop Thomas Becket in Canterbury Cathedral. Becket had fallen out with King Henry II, whose friends behaved in very unchristian ways. Becket had excommunicated them. One night king and bishop argued furiously and Henry shouted the immortal words 'Will no one rid me of this troublesome priest?' Horrified at what he had done in the heat of the moment, Sir William spent the rest of his life buttering up a furious Pope and trying to atone for his evil deed.

THE BLACK DEATH

The Black Death of 1348 killed over a quarter of England's population and had a particularly bad impact in Devon. Symptoms included black buboes (lumps) in the neck, groin or under arms, fever and vomiting black liquid. We now know that the plague was transmitted by fleas that had bitten infected rats, but this was not understood until hundreds of years later. Most people died within a week. Exeter lost nearly two-thirds of its inhabitants. This was possibly due to the fact that the city was mostly enclosed within its ancient walls, which while keeping possible plague victims out, allowed the disease to spread inside the city. One person who did escape was Bishop Grandisson, who left Exeter for the remote countryside. You could argue that he did the only sensible thing, but he left his clergymen to it and many of them caught the plague while trying to comfort those dying from it. The death toll meant that in the country there were not enough people to grow crops or look after livestock. Business in towns could not be carried out because people with the skills needed had often died of the plague themselves. Businesses affected included farming, fishing, government mining and trade. A plus point was that formerly downtrodden workers could expect better pay.

Grandisson sent word to the Bishop of Winchester, asking to borrow priests to replace those who had died. The Winchester priests refused to go!

Of Castles and Kings

Medieval rulers in Britain were big on castle building to subdue the natives. In Devon powerful local families built their own castles. Okehampton Castle was built in 1068 by Baldwin Fitzgilbert, a friend of King William. It is a motte and bailey castle. A motte is a large earthwork that gave the castle a good defensive position. A bailey is an enclosure with walls and buildings inside. Today, Okehampton Castle is a picturesque ruin. Tiverton Castle was built in 1106, in a good position overlooking the strategic River Exe. It was once home to the Earls of Devon but was later converted into a large country house. There are a pair of resident ghosts – a man and his dog who were killed in a fight about a woman! Marisco Castle was built in 1243 on Lundy Island by Henry III. Lundy had been lawless under the pirate William de Marisco and King Henry tried to stop him. This didn't work – Marisco wanted the King murdered to stop his interference in the contraband trade. Marisco was eventually captured, hanged, drawn and quartered.

Powderham Castle, built in the 1300s at Kenton near Exeter, is actually a fortified manor house. Parts date back to the 1300s but there have been many additions. Powderham has belonged to the Earls of Devon for generations. It is one of the most haunted castles in Britain. The creepiest ghost is the Grey Lady, a severe children's nanny from the early 1800s. Today she has often upset visitors' guide dogs!

Dartmouth Castle was built in 1388 by John Hawley at the mouth of the strategic River Dart. Dartmouth itself is a deep water port and the castle warded off attacks by pirates and later by the French during the Hundred Years' War. John Hawley was a privateer – allowed to plunder the ships of England's enemies. He became Mayor of Dartmouth fourteen times and was a rich land owner. In 1404 he defeated a large French raiding party at Slapton Sands.

In the late 1380s Geoffrey Chaucer wrote the famous *Canterbury Tales* about a diverse group of people on a pilgrimage to Canterbury Cathedral. He based his character the Shipman of Dartmouth on John Hawley after meeting him in the town and hearing about his adventures.

THE GROWTH OF TOWNS

During the later medieval period, settlements that had been no more than tiny villages began to grow, becoming important market towns due to the trade in tin, wool and other produce. Trading towns included Exeter, Barnstaple, Tavistock, Ashburton, Lydford, Chagford and Plympton.

From a fishing village, Plymouth grew during the late medieval period and became a craft town and trading port. This was helped by a rule that stated anyone going on a pilgrimage had to leave via Plymouth. Its strategic position was noted by the French, who during one war or another attacked and seriously damaged the town on several occasions.

Dartmouth also became a major Devon port and an important town. This was partly due to its naturally deep harbour, which needed no alteration to allow large ships in. As well as trading vessels, Dartmouth was an early naval port. Many crusaders on their way to the Holy Land left from Dartmouth.

The Rise of Fishing Villages

The village of Clovelly has the steepest street in Devon, which drops 880 yards to the harbour. Building a village on such a steep incline would be a challenging engineering project today but incredibly, many of the buildings date back to the late medieval era. The main street still has no access for vehicles. Beer has been a fishing village from at least the medieval era and is still thriving today. Seaton also has a fishing industry. Other fishing villages include Ilfracombe, which was once also a port for anyone wanting to travel north by boat.

Important Bridges

Due to the success of trade, industry and commerce, there were improvements in the number and quality of roads in the county during the late medieval period. More roads meant that more bridges were built to span rivers.

Clyst St Mary Bridge is probably the oldest of its kind still in existence in Devon. The bridge spans the River Clyst and is still used today, having been kept in good condition.

Exeter's medieval bridge was built in the late twelfth century over the River Exe and was the main way into the city. In its heyday the bridge had buildings along it but only part of the structure remains today. A walk on the bridge is still possible. Over the centuries the route of the river has changed and the bridge is now high and dry. This often puzzles visitors who, not unreasonably, expect to see the river under it!

The Clapper Bridge at Postbridge on Dartmoor was built in around 1370. It is located in a popular tourist area and hundreds of people walk over it in the summer, marvelling at the huge stone slabs used in its construction.

Bideford Long Bridge over the River Torridge was built in 1474 and has twenty-four arches. Wealthy people subscribed and each had an arch built. The more they paid, the bigger their arch! They varied from around 12 to 25ft. Bideford Bridge is one of the longest medieval bridges in England – an odd feat of engineering.

The Cocky Countess

Countess Isabella de Fortibus was a medieval woman who, unusually, was in charge of her own life and refused to follow the herd! She was born in 1237 and was the daughter of Baldwin de Redvers, the powerful Earl of Devon. When her brother died she became her father's heir. Aged 12, she married wealthy William de Fortibus and had six children before her husband died young. William's wealth was added to her already bulging coffers as her children were minors.

Isabella spent the rest of her life avoiding marriage proposals, though her family tried to push her into matrimony. She remained determinedly single and independent, outliving all of her children. Isabella's undoubted ruthless streak is shown by the fact that from around 1280 she was responsible for ruining Exeter's port and salmon fishery. She did this by building a weir across the River Exe below Exeter. This stopped ships reaching the city and affected salmon spawning. Topsham, near the Exe estuary, became the major port and a very wealthy town, and Isabella had a controlling interest! It was over 250 years until the situation was rectified.

Exeter's Underground Passages

A major project in Exeter was begun in the 1220s – a water supply leading from a natural well outside the city to Cathedral Close. In the 1340s a new cathedral water supply was built. Passages made from purple volcanic stone contained the pipes, allowing easy access for repair. Later sections of passage were built using Heavitree stone. This time St Nicholas Priory and the city had a third share each. A fountain in Cathedral Close gave access to the water. The oldest part of the passages that visitors can see today on a guided tour comes from this period. In 1420 another water supply with access passages was built, supplying Exeter citizens. The 'City Passage' ran under the High Street to a fountain, called The Great Conduit, at the top of Fore Street. In 1492 another section was built from outside the city.

The End of the Middle Ages

The Wars of the Roses were a series of civil wars fought between two royal houses with claims to the throne of England. The Lancastrians' emblem was a red rose and the Yorkist house adopted a white rose as its badge. The wars lasted from 1455 until August 1485 when Henry Tudor, Earl of Richmond, defeated Yorkist King Richard III at the Battle of Bosworth Field. Henry became the first Tudor King of England.

Prophetic!

In 1483 King Richard III visited Exeter when touring his realm. He had taken his nephew Edward's throne after the boy and his brother disappeared in the Tower of London. One popular theory is that Richard had the boys murdered.

In local legend, referenced in Shakespeare's *Richard III*, Exeter officials worried that Richard was bored with his visit. Then he noticed Rougemont Castle. He was taken to see it and found it interesting. On being told that the castle's name was 'Rougemont', Richard began to shake and moan. He fell to his knees gasping. Then someone mentioned the name again. Richard's recovery was instant. He'd mistaken the name 'Rougemont' for 'Richmond', the name of his bitter rival Henry. A witch had told him that two years after seeing 'Richmond', Richard would die. Two years later the Earl of Richmond, Henry Tudor, became Henry VII after killing Richard in battle.

10

THE TUDORS: RELIGION AND SEAFARING

HENRY VII (1457–1509)

After the upheavals of the Norman period, Henry VII stabilised the country, even marrying Elizabeth of York, a niece of his enemy Richard III, to do so. Henry combined the red rose of his house, the Lancastrians, with dead King Richard's Yorkist white rose to form the red and white 'Tudor Rose', but there was more trouble to come.

THE PERKIN WARBECK REBELLION

Perkin Warbeck was born in France in the 1470s into an ordinary family. He looked like Prince Richard of York, one of the princes in the tower. The French nobility encouraged Warbeck to claim to be Richard to destabilise England. Some people in England believed he was the prince as well. Warbeck tried to land in England in the early 1590s, but he and his supporters were held off and left without a fight. In 1496, though, he managed to get to Devon. His resemblance to Richard gained him support and an army was raised. Faced with fighting professional soldiers, Warbeck dithered. He was captured, sent to the Tower of London (ironically where the real Prince Richard was possibly killed) and executed in 1499.

For bravely defending Exeter against Warbeck's attack, grateful King Henry presented the loyal town with his sword and Cap of Maintenance – a sign of high honour. They are still brought out for special ceremonies today.

Henry VIII (1491–1547)

Ruthless, bad tempered and loud, Henry VIII became King because his elder brother, Arthur, Prince of Wales, died. He then married Arthur's widow, Katherine. Henry's lack of a male heir caused him to divorce her. Five more wives followed, producing Princess Mary, Princess Elizabeth and finally a sickly prince Edward. Henry was ruthless in his pursuit of a male heir. He needed one to keep the country stable and avoid the disruption and warfare of the Middle Ages. Henry fell out with the Pope because of his divorces. This led to England's reformation and the adoption of Protestantism. The Pope excommunicated Henry.

The Dissolution of the Monasteries

In 1536 Henry began the dissolution of Catholic monasteries. His henchmen raided the buildings for money and valuables, which Henry took. In Devon, he dissolved many religious institutions including: St Nicholas Priory, Exeter, founded in 1087, which was turned into a grand house; Torre Abbey, founded 1196, which was partly demolished but is now restored; Tavistock Abbey, founded in the 970s, which was given to Sir John Russel and today is mostly ruins; Plymouth Greyfriars, founded in 1383 and has little remaining; Buckland Abbey, founded in 1278 and sold to Sir Francis Drake, who turned it into a fine house; Cornworthy Priory, founded in 1205 and now a ruin; Newnham Abbey, founded in 1246 and bought from Henry VIII by Thomas Howard, uncle of Catherine Howard, Henry's fifth wife, whom the King had executed. As well as the cultural vandalism, the poorer in society suffered because many of these places had cared for the sick and needy and provided education.

Edward VI (1537–53)

Edward VI became King at the age of 9 when his father Henry died. He was the first English monarch brought up from birth as a Protestant. When he became King he was surrounded by fervently Protestant advisors.

The Prayer Book Rebellion

In 1549 the Book of Common Prayer came into use. This was in English, rather than the Latin of Catholic Services. It would be fair to assume that ordinary people would be happy with this. After all, only educated wealthy people studied Latin properly and a prayer book in English would be better for everyone. But some people in Devon were outraged by the change. At Sampford Courtenay on Whit Sunday, the first day the new prayer book came into use, there was a lot of anger. Outside the church there were bitter arguments. Insults were shouted and a farmer, William Hellyons, was shot and killed, starting a rebellion. Protesters, many of them armed with only pitchforks and sticks, marched 25 miles to Exeter, gathering support on the way. At Exeter the rebels were defeated by the Army, who were far better equipped. Thousands were killed in the rebellion and surviving ringleaders were executed.

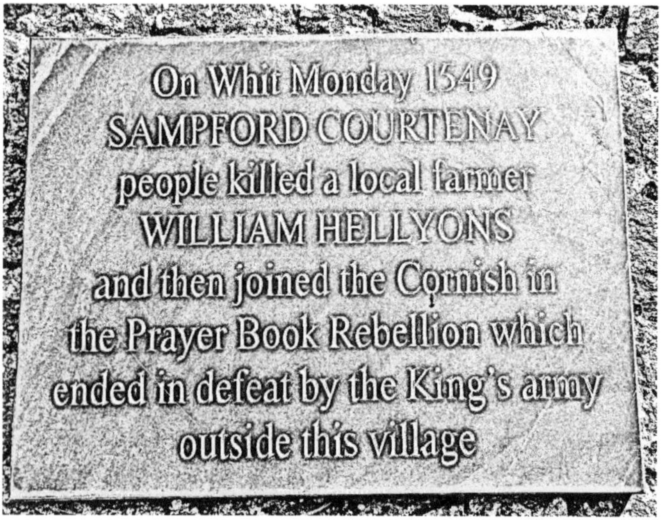

MARY I (1516–58)

'Bloody' Queen Mary resented the fact that her father, Henry, had cast off her mother. Mary became an ardent Catholic at odds with her father's religion. As Mary had no children, the crown eventually passed to her Protestant sister, who became Queen Elizabeth I.

RELIGIOUS PERSECUTION

Mary persecuted Protestants. In five years over 300 were burned at the stake, mostly in the Home Counties. Devon did not escape this cruelty. Agnes Prest, a staunch but carefully private Protestant, was betrayed to the authorities by her Catholic husband. Agnes was simple and didn't have the wit to defend herself. She was burned at the stake at Southernhay, Exeter, in 1557. The area was also used for hangings. Today there are beautiful public gardens at the scene. Bloody Mary richly deserves her nickname but her father, Henry VIII, also had a man, Thomas Benet, executed in Exeter for his religious beliefs. This was while Henry was still a Catholic. Benet was not impressed by Catholicism, especially where priests had lax morals. He nailed anti-Catholic posters to Exeter Cathedral door and was executed by burning. There is a memorial to Agnes Prest and Thomas Benet in Denmark Road, Exeter.

The Wyatt Rebellion

The Wyatt Rebellion occurred because some people objected to Queen Mary's marriage to Philip of Spain. The rebellion was led by Thomas Wyatt from Kent but Edward Courtenay, Earl of Devon, and Peter Carew, MP for Tavistock, were also involved. It was suspected that Princess Elizabeth, her sister's potential rival to the throne, might have been involved in setting up the rebellion, but nothing could be proved, or maybe it was a case of Mary not wanting to upset Protestants by punishing Protestant Elizabeth! Parliament had suggested that Englishman Courtenay would make Mary a suitable husband, but she would have none of it and insisted on marriage to Phillip. Anti-Catholics were outraged. Not only was Phillip the wrong religion, but he was Spanish! People from all backgrounds were not happy about this turn of events and Mary's advisors, who were being ignored, were furious. The rebellion didn't really get under way in Devon though.

When it finally collapsed, Wyatt, as the ringleader, was executed. Carew was imprisoned and Courtenay was exiled.

They were both lucky not to have been severely punished long before this as they had each tried to court Princess (later Queen) Elizabeth and Mary at the same time. Two-timing a royal princess, especially when it was with her sister, was not a good idea!

Never Such Devoted Sisters

Berry Pomeroy Castle was built in the Tudor period for the Seymour family. At first glance, the structure is puzzling – the castle is built inside the ruins of a much older building. Berry Pomeroy is picturesque in a very creepy way. It has a lot of ghost stories, including one about a beautiful Tudor lady, the daughter of the owner. She was murdered by her much plainer sister, who was trying to pinch her wealthy husband to be. Berry Pomeroy is claimed to be the most haunted building in Britain.

Berry Pomeroy castle clergymen tended to live to great ages. At least six served as personal vicar, one after the other, to the family for more than fifty years each. This was in the Tudor and Stuart eras when many people didn't even live to the age of 50!

Chocolate Box

This term describes a pretty building of the sort seen on chocolate box lids. Devon has many, mostly made of cob. Making cob was not pretty! It consisted of water soil, straw and lime, which all had to be mixed together and plastered on over a framework. The material was first used in construction in ancient times. It remained popular in Devon into the late Tudor period. Traditionalists with a cob house (even if it is a more modern version) usually paint the plastered outside walls in pink, cream or white. Cob buildings in any other colour still annoy purists!

Guildhalls

Guildhalls are traditionally buildings where guilds could meet, and where council meetings and other official gatherings take place. A number of towns in Devon have guildhalls. Among the earliest are two with parts dating from the Tudor period. In Exeter there has been a civic building on the site of the Guildhall for 800 years. It was used as a prison, a court of law, for guild business and as council chambers. The front of the building dates from the 1590s and has an upper floor that juts out over the pavement on pillars. The imposing structure made people take notice of this important civil building. The huge front door is awe inspiring. Made of thick, heavily carved oak, it was installed by a local builder in the 1590s. Inside are impressive curved oak roof supports and panelling. It is said that Exeter Guildhall is the oldest municipal building still in use in the country. In 1553, King Edward VI allowed Totnes to have a guildhall. Over the years the building has been used as a prison and a school. In 1646 it was used by Oliver

Cromwell, who discussed military tactics there as the building had large tables for unrolling maps.

TUDOR INNS OR INNS IN TUDOR BUILDINGS!

There are lots of inns in Devon and many that are all or partly Tudor (I could write a book ...!). Here are a few that are either historically interesting, atmospheric, beautiful, or all three:

The Hole in the Wall Pub, Torquay, was once a haunt of smugglers and pirates. It has been a pub since the 1540s and is tucked away on a narrow plot that gives the building a curiously triangular appearance.

The Minerva Inn is one of Plymouth's oldest. It has the aged black beams and tiny Tudor windowpanes you might expect to see. It also has something you might not expect – a ghostly lady in Tudor dress!

Cowick Barton Inn, Exeter was once part of a priory. The building was converted into a mansion in the 1540s and later became an inn. Inside there are a lot of Tudor features. Witchcraft is suspected after very old bones of several species of animal were discovered by builders under floorboards in recent times.

The Hartland Quay Hotel and Pub is next to a quay that was built for the transportation of goods. The building was once a malt house. It is in the most amazing location, with jagged rocks and rough sea to the front and incredible natural rock folds to one side caused by intense pressure millions of years ago.

Queen Elizabeth I (1558–1603)

Elizabeth reigned for almost forty-five years. At various times during her childhood, Henry VIII declared her illegitimate. Yet the well-educated, tolerant (for her time), brave and single-minded Elizabeth's reign was a great success. This was partly due to her refusal to marry. As she herself said, 'I already have a husband and that is the Kingdom of England!' The Queen had many male favourites among her courtiers however, and some of these had connections with Devon. In Elizabeth's reign Devon became particularly important due to its various seafaring activities.

Pirates and Explorers

Many of England's most famous explorers at this time were from Devon. In Elizabethan times the terms 'piracy' and 'exploration' were interchangeable. The Queen herself was known to turn a blind eye, particularly when the piracy was against her enemies, the Spanish. Walter Raleigh, born in 1552 at East Budleigh, was one of Elizabeth's favourite seafarers and pirates. It may have helped that he was supposed to be very good looking.

After Oxford University, Raleigh went to sea. Among the places he visited was South America looking for the city of gold, El Dorado. He didn't find it because it was a myth.

Raleigh continued to be a favourite of the Queen until he married without permission, which was a no-no at court in those days! Elizabeth forgave him, but her successor, King James, was not so forgiving. He had Raleigh executed for plotting against him.

- Unfortunately the famously gallant image of Raleigh throwing his cloak over a puddle to stop Queen Elizabeth getting muddy feet is almost certainly a myth.

- Raleigh may have been the first person to bring potatoes from South America to England. Despite the legend, though, he was almost certainly not the person responsible for bringing tobacco to these shores. This was down to Plymouth seafarer John Hawkins in 1573.

- In 1585 Raleigh had a colony established in America. This was called Roanoke, in an area called Virginia (after the virgin queen, Elizabeth). The settlers all disappeared!

John Hawkins, born in 1532, raided many Spanish ships for valuables. These included Africans who were sold into slavery, sadly considered acceptable back then. Hawkins was among the senior sailors involved in defeating the Spanish Armada.

Sir Francis Drake was born in 1540 in Tavistock. Drake was more of an explorer, who circumnavigated the world between 1577 and 1580. He and his crew were the first to try this and get back alive. In 1581 he became Mayor of Plymouth and was known for charitable work and town improvements such as the construction of a freshwater system known as

'Drake's Leat'. This brought water from the River Meavy into Plymouth over 12 miles. It was lined with granite slabs. Many people, while grateful for the water supply that Drake had built, suspected that he was a witch. Legend says that when Drake was dying he claimed that his drum would start to beat itself if England was in danger from enemies. Drake would then come back to life and save the nation. Over the years various people claim to have heard the drum, but not seen Drake! In life he was too powerful for witchcraft accusations to stick. He actually accused several others of practising witchcraft. Drake had one of his senior naval officers, Thomas Doughty, executed for it on trumped-up evidence because Doughty, a very experienced sailor, had questioned some of Drake's voyage plans.

- Drake bought Buckland Abbey and turned it into a grand house complete with deer park. Unfortunately this swashbuckling sailor found that he was scared of stags!
- Almost certainly, Drake didn't insist on finishing his game of bowls on Plymouth Hoe after learning of the approach of the Spanish Armada.

THE SPANISH ARMADA: BROTHER AND SISTER-IN-LAW AT WAR!

The Armada took place thirty years after the death of King Phillip's wife, Queen Mary of England, the Catholic half-sister of Elizabeth I.

Sir Francis Drake led the English fleet against the Spanish Armada in 1588. The Armada was ordered by King Phillip II. It left Lisbon at the end of May and was first seen by the English off the coast of Cornwall. The Spanish had 130 ships and 27,000 men, while the English had 100 ships and 10,000 men. As well as Vice Admiral Drake, the English fleet was commanded by Admiral Lord Howard and Rear Admiral John Hawkins. Spain's ships anchored in Calais. Here Drake's expert tactics assisted the English victory. He sent fire ships into Calais harbour, which burned some of the Spanish vessels. The sea battle of Gravelines helped to defeat Spain. Many Spanish ships were sunk or were wrecked on the English coast. It is believed that descendants of these survivors still live in Devon and Cornwall.

Exeter's old Ship Inn claims to have been Drake's favourite pub. A quote outside begins, 'Next to my own shippe I do most love that old Shippe in Exon.' Stunning Mols Coffeehouse nearby was apparently where he planned what to do if the Spanish navy invaded. A nice story, but why come all the way to Exeter to do it?

Smuggling

Picturesque Appledore in north Devon is popular with visitors, who enjoy strolling along the harbour or among the quaint old cottages that once housed the town's fishing fleet and its fishermen. Few would imagine Appledore's villainous past! From the Elizabethan era the town was famous for its smuggling. Tobacco was a major commodity and almost certainly the poor fishermen were involved. Those narrow streets of tiny fishermen's cottages were ideal for hiding ill-gotten gains.

Newfoundland Cod Fishing

At Newfoundland Island off the east coast of Canada, cod fishing had become very lucrative by Elizabeth's reign and involved many Devon seamen. Cod fishing in the freezing conditions was hard and dangerous work, and involved many months at sea, but it was well paid. The seas off Newfoundland can still be treacherous for modern ships, never mind wooden sailing ships. Sadly, modern overfishing has all but ruined the trade.

Exeter, as a trading port, was struggling because of the weirs built by Isabela de Fortibus. Petitions to subsequent kings didn't seem to make any difference. Then in the 1560s permission for a change was granted and engineer John Trew was employed to circumnavigate the weirs by building a canal alongside the river. This allowed ships to discharge and pick up cargoes from Exeter. The canal is over 3 miles long and was the first to have pound locks. These allow boats to manoeuvre from one part of the canal to another, where the water is higher or lower. Exeter's maritime trade continued until the 1960s. Today the canal and quay are an important pleasure area for tourists and Exeter people.

Lace Manufacturing

The art of hand-making lace probably began in Europe. By Queen Elizabeth's reign it was well established in Devon, where it became known as 'Honiton Lace' as the town was a major producer. Honiton lace seems to have become popular because Queen Elizabeth so obviously liked it! Many paintings of her show lace-trimmed ruff collars and dresses, and where the Queen led, her courtiers and the aristocracy all over England (female and male) followed.

As lace making was such a slow, elaborate art, only the wealthy could afford it.

CIDER

Making cider is an ancient art. Some say that growing apples for the purpose pre-dates the Roman invasion, but the Romans are known to have brought apple trees with them. There was a slump in cider manufacturing after the Black Death as there was in most industries due to lack of manpower. By the Elizabethan era though, cider had become important again, and still is! Traditional cider production methods used a moving press made of heavy wood or stone, which would grind the apples and squeeze out the juice. Apple cider vinegar – made from fermenting apple peelings, sugar and water – is a traditional cold remedy that actually works and is still used by many people today.

A more serious illness that cider vinegar definitely couldn't cure was the Black Death. Well, if the plague got you, at least you would be spared any more of this revolting concoction!

Crediton, in the heart of cider country, had a number of outbreaks of the plague in the Elizabethan era. It is possible that the disease was brought to the town by travelling traders who went to Crediton to sell their goods at the market. The plague hit Crediton particularly badly in 1571, when several hundred people died. This was a lot for a small town. In 1591 and into the 1600s the plague returned, although probably not as seriously.

SOME MORE IMPORTANT TUDOR BUILDINGS

The Merchant's House in Plymouth is a beautiful Elizabethan town house built of limestone with timber-work. The house was once owned by William Parker, a mayor of the town during Elizabeth's reign. The Butterwalk in Dartmouth was a row of merchants' houses. The upper floor was supported on pillars with a covered 'walk' beneath. The building, like many Tudor ones, has some improbable angles! The Great House, Tiverton, was once the home of wealthy Tudor merchant George Slee. The house is built of beautiful mellow red sandstone. Slee was a caring and popular individual who founded alms houses for the relief of the poor of Tiverton.

Exeter's beautiful black and white 'Merchant's House' is more intriguingly known as the 'House That Moved'. In 1961 it was decided that the house had to be demolished to make way for a new road. Local people were aghast. After protests to the council, it was decided that the whole house should be moved. It was clad in wood and carefully lifted onto a low loader, which was winched nearly 300ft to its present location on Frog Street. The move took three days to complete and involved some anxious moments. But the house was saved.

The 'House That Moved'

11

THE EARLY STUARTS: THE TROUBLE WITH RELIGION

JAMES I (1566–1625)

Protestant James I was the son of Mary, Queen of Scots. He inherited the crown of England from Elizabeth I, and the throne of Scotland (as James VI) from his mother, whom Elizabeth had executed. This united England and Scotland. James believed that he held supremacy over the church. He also believed in the Divine Right of Kings, meaning only God had authority over him.

REMEMBER, REMEMBER THE FIFTH OF NOVEMBER ...

Catholics hoped that James I would tolerate their faith, but he didn't. The Gunpowder Plot was hatched by Catholic Guy Fawkes and others. They put thirty-six barrels of gunpowder in the cellar of the Houses of Parliament. The intention was to blow it up, and many influential Protestants with it. However, the plot was discovered and the conspirators were tortured, hanged, drawn and quartered.

Deodand was an ancient law that was still practised in superstitious Devon in the reign of James I. The law stated that the devil was responsible when any object caused the death of a person. Often the offending item was destroyed because it 'Had the Devil within it'. Not only was this wasteful, but unfortunate animals often fell victim to the superstition. The practice didn't fully die out until the 1800s.

Pilgrim Fathers

Plymouth was a small fishing town until the popularity of pilgrimages to other countries began. From the 1400s, hundreds set off on sea voyages from Plymouth to European religious centres. The most famous, the Pilgrim Fathers, left Plymouth in July 1620 on the *Mayflower*. They travelled to what is now known as America. The pilgrims had been unhappy about the intolerance of the Protestant Church and the sin in English society. After a long and stormy voyage, the Pilgrims landed in the New World. While at sea a pilgrim died and another was born. The new baby was called Oceanus Hopkins. The pilgrims established New Plymouth near modern Boston. Many died from cold, disease and lack of food in the first years, but they began to make it work. Celebrations of the 400th anniversary took place in Plymouth in 2020.

Lots of tourists to Plymouth make their way to the 'Mayflower Steps' at the harbour leading down to the sea. Sadly, these are not the steps used by the Pilgrim Fathers. The original ones are buried under a Victorian pub.

The Pilgrim Steps, Plymouth

12

THE CIVIL WAR: COUNTY IN TURMOIL

The English Civil War was in three parts. Parts one (1642–46) and two (1648–49) ended with the defeat of Charles I and his execution at Whitehall, London on 30 January 1649. Part three (1649–51) began when Charles II was declared King by his supporters. It ended with the defeat of Charles II and his escape to France.

CHARLES I (1600–49)

King Charles I, son of James I, was unpopular. His wife, Henrietta Maria, was a Catholic. Worse still, Charles had Catholic leanings. He was another King who believed in the Divine Right of Kings. In 1629 he dissolved parliament but later restored it because he wanted money to invade Scotland. Parliament refused him, so Charles put up taxes instead. This upset a lot of the population and led to unrest. Parliament put the Army under its control. The ensuing Civil War lasted nine years.

The Wars Begin

In January 1643, three north Devon leaders of the Parliamentarian forces, Sir John Northcote, Sir Samuel Rolle and Sir John Bampfield, raised a force of over 9,000 men with the aim of reinforcing their troops at Plymouth. Many of the new north Devon 'soldiers' were in fact farmers who were more or less forced into military service. Such groups were known as 'clubmen' because they had no guns and were, at first, armed with clubs, or farm tools. These men suffered serious deprivation during the war, as ordinary soldiers always have.

Some First Civil War Battles in Devon 1642–46

Like other areas of the country, there were many sieges and battles great and small in Civil War Devon, with many places affected. The Royalists fought for Charles and the Parliamentarians under Oliver Cromwell. Main Civil War battles in Devon include:

Barnstaple

Barnstaple supported the Parliamentarians, but the town changed hands four times during the Civil War! Many people in the town had a beef with King Charles I because he had resurrected an old stealth tax whereby towns near the coast had to pay quite significant annual sums for the build and maintenance of naval vessels. The practice was known as 'ship money'. In 1643 Barnstaple was taken by Royalist Prince Maurice. The Parliamentary forces were low on ammunition and there was sickness in the town.

Barnstaple fell for the last time after the Parliamentary forces took over in 1646 after a long siege.

EXETER

Like many wealthy towns, Exeter suffered under the tax demands of Charles I. Exeter's city walls were repaired and strengthened, and defensive earth banks and ditches were built. The Parliamentarians managed to withstand attempts by the Royalists to take the city. Exeter Cathedral was badly damaged by Puritan Parliamentarian troops, who committed acts of vandalism and stole valuables. They disapproved of the adornment and 'high church' principles to be found in many religious establishments. In 1643, Royalist forces took Exeter. In April 1644, Henrietta Maria, wife of King Charles I, was on her way to safety in France – her home country. She was very pregnant and stayed at Bedford House in Exeter to rest. On 17 June she gave birth to a daughter, Henrietta Anne. Her father King Charles I saw her only once when he visited Exeter. She and her mother went to France. Henrietta Anne's turbulent start in life didn't get much easier. While living in France she married Philip Duke of Orleans when she was aged 16. It was not a happy union. Philip was jealous, unfaithful and uncaring. Henrietta Anne died aged 26, possibly poisoned on her husband's orders. A painting of the ill-fated young woman hangs in Exeter Guildhall.

When King Charles I visited his wife and baby in Exeter, he ordered that local musicians should accompany him into the town and remain to entertain him. Very few turned up, expecting that they might be caught in the crossfire if the Parliamentarians tried an attack.

In 1645 the Royalists, expecting Parliamentarian forces, demolished a lot of Exeter buildings. This was done to allow Royalists unrestricted lines of fire. It didn't work. In 1646 Exeter was once more in Parliamentary hands in time for the end of the war.

It is said that Exeter's White Hart was where Oliver Cromwell stabled his horses while he was in the town. Today the stables are part of the reception, but there are still iron mangers and other artefacts to be seen. Cromwell may well have stayed at the inn himself and there is even a 'Cromwell Suite'. However, most towns seem to have an inn where Cromwell stayed!

Much to his annoyance, while on military manoeuvres, King Charles had to stay the night in a common pub along with common people in the village of Bow, some miles from Exeter. This was because there was nowhere in the area posh enough for him! This is not to say that there is anything wrong with Bow, rather that Charlie was a snob.

Plymouth

Plymouth was besieged almost continually by the Royalists, who were after control of its port. Defences built by Henry VIII were quickly repaired and added to, with all able-bodied people lending a hand. In 1643, Royalists attacked Plymouth in the dark and succeeded in gaining entry, but they got lost. They stumbled to a beach, where they were cut off by the tide.

In the Civil War era, many of Devon's roads were rough tracks. People in out-of-the-way communities were very isolated and hardly travelled. Two years into the Civil War, a farmer was puzzled to see soldiers near his tiny homestead. On being told that there was going to be a battle between the Parliamentary and Royalist forces, the farmer was amazed. He hadn't known the war was still on!

TIVERTON

Tiverton was a Royalist town. Its castle was a stronghold for Royalist troops based in the area. It suffered a major outbreak of deadly typhus that killed many soldiers and civilians, but they continued to hold out against the Parliamentarians. Worse was to come though. By a strange thousand to one fluke, the Parliamentarians managed to gain entry into the strongly fortified castle. During heavy firing, a Parliamentarian soldier managed to hit the castle gate, shearing the metal holding the gate shut.

SOURTON

Sourton, near Okehampton, is a quiet village, picturesquely set on the northern edge of Dartmoor. It is popular with walkers as they make their way up to Sourton Tor and the remains of the stone circle. On 25 April 1643 the peace of Sourton was shattered when a battle took place between the Royalists and Parliamentarians. To begin with the Royalists, covered by the rocks of the tor, looked like they would win. Then the Parliamentarians gained the upper hand, forcing their enemies to flee. If you decide on a walk to the tors and happen to be coming back at dusk, you may hear ghostly cries and the clashing of metal. Or so some people claim!

Ilfracombe

This town supported the Parliamentarians. At one stage in the war, a few Royalists made a minor incursion when they damaged property and looted. This may well have been ordinary troops looking for food. They were soon chased away. Later in the war the Royalists did get the town again, but only briefly. In a last push towards victory Parliamentarians advanced on Ilfracombe again. All was up for the Royalists in the town because requested reinforcements failed to arrive!

Modbury

Located in south Devon, the market town of Modbury had two Civil War battles to contend with! The place is quiet today and would have been much smaller and quieter in 1600. So why, then, was it fought over twice? The answer to this is provisions. Modbury is in an agricultural area and troops need feeding.

Battle number one took place on 9 December 1642. From Totnes, Parliamentary forces moved to Kingsbridge and took the Auton Gifford Bridge, strategically important as a route into the food production areas. This time the Royalists won.

Battle number two was on 21 February 1643. This time the hungry Parliamentarians were ready. Their forces heavily outnumbered the Royalists, many of whom fled to Cornwall to regroup with their forces there.

Chagford

The Three Crowns Inn at Chagford was the location of the death of Royalist poet soldier and MP Sydney Godolphin. Had he lived beyond the age of 33 he may have become a major poet. He was shot while seeking cover in the building.

For some reason he had joined the Royalist Army as an ordinary soldier although his family was wealthy and he could have had a commission. The Three Crowns Inn is on an ordinary, quiet village street and gives a real feel of how close the combat was.

Prince Maurice of Palatine (1621–52) was a nephew of Charles I and served the Royalist side during the Civil War. In October 1643 he took Dartmouth, establishing a strong force. Ancient earthworks outside the town were used to position a large number of guns and cannons to protect the town from attack by the Parliamentarians. Prince Maurice reviewed troops in Crediton at Lords Meadow, which would have been near the site of today's Lords Meadow Leisure Centre.

Great Torrington

Great Torrington was one of the last Royalist strongholds in the Civil War. The town was small, but over 17,000 soldiers were involved in the fighting, which was particularly fierce. Winning the upper hand, Parliamentarians imprisoned nearly 200 Royalist troops in the Church of St Michael and All Angels in the centre of Great Torrington on 16 February 1646. You might think that they were safe there. Not so. An earlier group of Royalists soldiers had hidden many barrels of gunpowder in the church basement for future use. The building was hit during the fighting, blowing all the prisoners to pieces and demolishing nearby buildings. The Parliamentarians claimed that they hadn't known

Civil War soldier's mass grave site, Great Torrington

that the gunpowder was there, but Royalists didn't believe them! Soon after Cromwell won the war, to make amends he had the church and other parts of the town rebuilt. The bodies of the dead Royalist soldiers are buried under a long stone-covered mound in the churchyard, where a plaque tells the grisly tale.

The defeat of the Royalists at Great Torrington was the beginning of the end of the first Civil War in Devon.

TWICE A TURNCOAT!

The Civil War caused a lot of death, destruction and anguish in England, but some people knew how to play the system. George Monck, a wealthy Army officer from Merton, Devon, began the Civil War fighting for King Charles I and the Royalist cause. He was captured by the Parliamentarians and, probably realising that the Royalists would be defeated, promptly switched sides, joining Cromwell's Parliamentarians. A good move, he must have thought, because Cromwell's army did win. When Cromwell died in 1658, Monck changed his mind and was a major supporter of Charles II when the monarchy was restored.

TOUGH SHOVE

Drake's Island off Plymouth was used as a prison for army officers who had fought for parliament in the Civil War. Under the orders of King Charles II, the men were kept in dreadful conditions. Unsurprisingly, Drake's Island is said to be haunted by the cries of the suffering Parliamentarians. It was claimed that some were pushed into the sea.

PLAGUE!

Just to heap a bit more misery on the people of Devon during the Civil War, they had a particularly nasty outbreak of the plague in 1645. As in other outbreaks, there were many quack 'cures' on offer to desperate people. These included rubbing plague buboes with a live chicken or dog,which was supposed to transfer the disease from the human victim to the animal; rubbing the victim with rotten human faeces (the smellier the better!); and eating marigold flowers mixed with egg shells.

Outbreaks of plague were relatively common in Devon and elsewhere in the 1500s and 1600s, with minor outbreaks often not even making news. Symptoms of bubonic plague usually began with an extreme fever alternating with chills. Severe diarrhoea followed, then swollen glands, gangrene turning the skin black and uncontrollable bleeding as the body broke down. The pneumonic version was even scarier. This affected the lungs and was passed to others on the breath of victims. This is written in the past tense, but bubonic plague still affects many areas of the world, although it can usually be cured using antibiotics.

The village of Zeal Monachorum did not get its name from the zeal with which it supported the monarchy during the Civil War! Zeal Monachorum had this name for centuries before the war began. One translation of the name is 'The Cell of Monks', meaning the rooms where monks slept.

The Second Civil War 1648–49

After Charles I's defeat in the first Civil War there was a lot of scrabbling for power between Charles' supporters and detractors, Scotland, the church and parliamentary supporters. This conflict hardly affected Devon. The brief Second Civil War ended with another parliamentary victory under General Fairfax. On 30 January 1649 Charles I was executed in London.

The Third Civil War 1649–51

Charles I's son, Charles II, had been sent to France. After his father's death, he was declared King Charles II by his supporters. He decided to invade England from Scotland, where he was also made king. Charles Junior was completely defeated by Parliamentarian forces at the Battle of Worcester. Expecting the same fate as his father, he went on the run to evade the Parliamentarians. There is a famous story about him hiding in a hollow oak tree while his enemies searched for him nearby without success.

An anti-Cromwell song, which was sung in Devon by supporters of Charles II, was:

> I'll bore a hole in Cromwell's nose,
> And therein put a string,
> And lead him up and down the town,
> For murdering Charles our king!

13

THE CROMWELLIAN ERA: POLITICAL CONUNDRUMS

Oliver Cromwell (1649–58)

Cromwell was the leading MP in the struggle to limit the power of King Charles I. He had become an MP in 1629. During the Civil War he proved himself to be a great military leader. He was among the first MPs to sign Charles I's death warrant.

The Short Parliament existed from April to May 1640. King Charles I was unable to persuade MPs to grant him money to fight Scotland. In a huff he dissolved parliament.

The Long Parliament kept going from 1640–60. It had been made more difficult to dissolve parliament unless the MPs agreed. They didn't. One in the eye for Charles!

The Rump Parliament was part of the Long Parliament. It would be amusing to think that someone had called MPs a lot of bottoms! Sadly, in this case 'rump' was an old name for 'remnant'. These were MPs who agreed to the execution of Charles I. Those that didn't had been thrown out. Of course, ordinary people would have had a good giggle at the term 'rump', no doubt!

Cromwell became Lord Protector of England and could have become king, but he refused, having no time for monarchs. He died in 1658.

Port towns such as Plymouth were growing larger and richer with the increase in trade. But more trade meant more piracy, and sometimes the pirates were daring and audacious in their attacks! In 1640 a Turkish pirate ship attacked a British trading vessel, the *Elizabeth*, in the English Channel itself – a risky business as other vessels could have been near enough to come to the *Elizabeth*'s aid. Unfortunately, this was not the case. Although the *Elizabeth*'s skilled crew managed to beat off the Turkish vessel, several passengers and crew were killed.

RICHARD CROMWELL (1658–60)

Richard was a second son. His older brother, Rupert, who would have taken over after his father, was killed in the Civil War. Richard was quiet and sensitive; he lacked the ability to control the Army and the Royalists grew stronger. Cromwell was removed (quite willingly) from his position as Lord Protector in May1659. Charles I's son was invited back from France to become Charles II. The new King, though, had no personal control of the army or government.

14

THE LATER STUARTS: MERRY MAKING AND MORE RELIGIOUS STRIFE

CHARLES II (1660–85)

Charles II became a popular king. He supported religious tolerance. He also liked a good time and was known as the 'Merry Monarch'. Theatres and other entertainments banned by Cromwell as ungodly opened again. But Charles is also known as the founder of the Royal Navy and the Royal Society, an institution of scientific learning.

Oliver Cromwell died twice ... Well, sort of. After Charles II became King, the usually tolerant monarch ordered that Cromwell should be disinterred and executed for high treason. His body was dug up, hanged and decapitated. His head was put on a long spike in public and remained there for years.

More Plague!

The village of Bradninch, being small, quiet and rural, is nothing like London. Right? Well, it does actually have something in common with the capital. In 1666 they both had 'Great Fires'. OK, London's conflagration caused the destruction of 13,000 buildings and Bradninch's losses amounted to a few hundred, but this was most of the village. There is another coincidence. In both places the replacement buildings were cleaner and, being new, easier to keep clean. This meant fewer rats. Neither London nor Bradninch ever had an outbreak of plague again.

Burials had taken place on Exeter's Cathedral Green since the 500s. Outbreaks of the plague in the 1300s began to fill Cathedral Green cemetery. By the 1600s coffins were being stacked on top of older ones, sometimes giving rise to a jumble of bones when earlier, rotting coffins gave way under the weight! Then bits of bone began to surface due to pressure from beneath. Cathedral clergymen and important visitors complained about the grisly spectacle. A man was then employed to check Cathedral Green each day and pull out any sticking-up bits of dead person.

Strategic Plymouth

Charles II understood the strategic, naval and military importance of Plymouth, and knew that other countries also understood! Charles was mindful of this, especially during the Dutch Wars of the 1660s, and the King realised that Plymouth needed better fortifications. In 1665 construction of Plymouth Royal Citadel began. Constructed of limestone, granite and Portland Stone, the structure is still impressive today. It towers over the Hoe and waterfront with walls over 70ft high and nearly ¼ mile long. It is still used as a military base.

WITCHCRAFT

Most people in Devon in the Stuart age were uneducated. Many lived in isolated communities where superstition and suspicion were rife. Perhaps it isn't surprising that many of these people believed in witches, given the upheavals, religious intolerance, violence and fear of those days. What is less easy to understand is that many educated people also believed in witches and that they deserved terrible and cruel treatment. Most 'witches' were elderly women. Many lived alone because they had no families. Unfortunately, as witches were believed to live by themselves, this caused suspicion. Some 'witches' may well have been senile and were accused of witchcraft because of their odd behaviour.

THE BIDEFORD WITCHES

Mary Trembles, Temperance Lloyd and Susannah Edwards: three poor women from Bideford who ticked all the boxes for suspicion of witchcraft. Furthermore, they were not shrinking violets! Instead they were loud and would answer anyone back including men (a no-no in those days) and their wealthy social 'betters'. In 1682 a Bideford woman named Grace Thomas accused Temperance Lloyd of witchcraft after feeling pins and needles all over her body after talking to Temperance. The unfortunate woman was questioned by the town's mayor and, acting in a confused manner, admitted the 'crime'. Under intense questioning she admitted that she had met the Devil, who was disguised as a black cat, and had taken him into Grace's bedroom while she slept. Temperance's

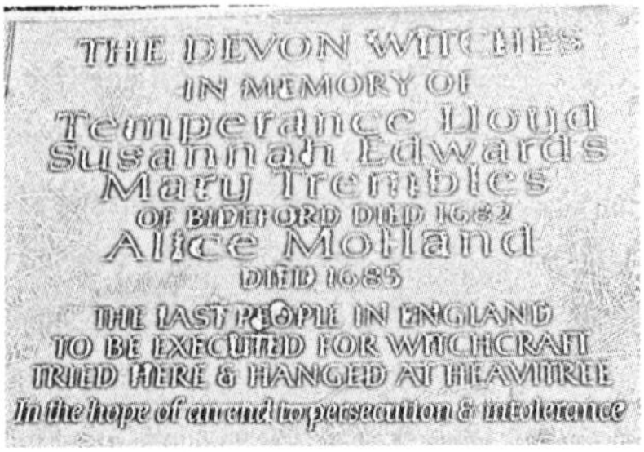

Memorial for the Bideford 'witches'

body was searched and 'unnatural teats' were found. These were probably skin tags. Accused of allowing the Devil to suckle from her, Temperance agreed that this had happened. She also confessed to causing shipwrecks by witchcraft.

Mary Trembles and Susanna Edwards had the misfortune to be friends of Temperance Lloyd. They were poor women who had to beg for food, and also lived alone. Mary and Susanna were accused of killing a woman by witchcraft when she refused to give them money or food. Other accusers claimed that the women had cast spells that made people ill and had caused livestock to die using witchcraft. The three women were tried at Exeter Castle Assizes in August 1682. Another Bideford woman accused of witchcraft was also executed in 1685 – the last person to suffer this fate in England. A plaque at Rougemont Castle in Exeter commemorates the unfortunate women.

Stand and Deliver

Exeter had its very own highwayman! John Barnes was the owner of an inn known as the Black Horse, which he ran from 1670. After a misspent youth he met a respectable religious lady and they married. Barnes was careful to have only well-behaved customers. As he was a very large man, he had no trouble ejecting anyone who got drunk, blasphemed or became lewd. Barnes and his wife had eight children and eventually they fell into debt. Too proud to ask friends for help, Barnes reverted to his criminal past and, with two accomplices, robbed a mail coach bound for London. They each stole £200, a fortune in those days. They may well have got away with the crime, but Barnes' giant frame stood out and he was recognised by a passenger on the coach. They were arrested, imprisoned and sentenced to death.

Rude Writer

The reign of Charles II seems a bit grim with witch persecution, piracy and violence, but the King enjoyed music, theatre and art, and these began to flourish. Exeter-born Thomas D'Ufrey originally trained as a lawyer but enjoyed entertaining his friends with naughty plays and songs. Eventually he moved to London, where King Charles enjoyed being lampooned in D'Ufrey's plays. Soon everybody who was anybody wanted to have the mickey taken out of them! Theatres were packed and the laughter of audiences was so loud that it could be heard from outside – a perfect contrast to the austerity of Cromwell's rule.

James II (1685–88)

The accession of James II didn't stop civil unrest. The new king was a Catholic (the last Catholic monarch in England). Worse still, he was intent on making the country Catholic again, too.

Monmouth Rebellion, May–June 1685

Enter James Duke of Monmouth, an illegitimate son of Charles II. In spite of his illegitimacy, which should have stopped him from becoming King, Charles decided to try to overthrow James II. In southern England, including Devon, there was a lot of support for Monmouth but many of his 'troops' were businessmen and farm workers without military training. After a few encounters with the regular army, Monmouth's cause was lost when he was defeated at the battle of Sedgemoor, Somerset. This was the last big battle in England. After the rebellion the infamous 'Hanging' Judge Jeffreys was called on to try rebels at a number of locations including Exeter Castle on 14 September 1685. Twelve ringleaders were hanged, drawn and quartered, while others were whipped. Many rebels were never caught as they either left the area or went into hiding.

Judge Jeffreys was known for the severity of his sentencing and for having a very bad temper! Jeffreys died aged 43, just four years after the Bloody Assizes. It is thought that he'd had a very painful and, then, untreatable kidney disease for several years. Perhaps this could explain his unpleasant personality!

Women's Writes

Lady Mary Chudleigh was born into a wealthy family in Winslade in 1656. She was a bright child but received only a very basic education. Like most wealthy parents, hers pushed her into a 'good' marriage when she was only 18. The marriage was very unhappy and Mary was frustrated by the lack of mental stimulation. Undaunted by her husband's disapproval, Mary began to write feminist articles and books. To the surprise of her family, her works found a publisher and began to make money! Legally any royalties would have gone to her husband, but he seems to have given up the fight against her 'unwomanly' behaviour. Her writing includes *The Ladies Defence, Or the Bride-Woman's Counsellor* in 1701, which warned of the adverse effects of marriage on women. In 1703, a book of poetry warned young women to maintain the support of female friends after marriage and only to marry for love.

William III and Mary II (1688–1702)

James II continued uneasily as King for another three years, but he was still at odds with parliament and Protestants and something had to give!

The Glorious Revolution

Princess Mary was the Protestant daughter of James II. She was married to William, Prince of Orange, Holland. By 1688, with nothing resolved regarding James II, parliament and influential nobles offered Mary the throne of England, to rule jointly with her husband.

William landed at Torbay on 4 November 1688, which happened to be his 38th birthday. His arrival marked the beginning of what is now known as the Glorious Revolution. But it very nearly didn't happen. William's fleet of ships encountered a severe storm on the way to England. This put several of them out of action and meant that people had to be transferred to other vessels. With William was an army of 2,000 experienced troops. Looks like he had learned from Monmouth's mistake of using farm labourers! Faced with a proper army, resistance was minimal. William wisely got the locals on side by making sure that they were generously paid for any provisions that his troops used. His army marched to several Devon towns, reaching Exeter on 8 November and collecting eager volunteers along the way. William allowed James to escape to France and this was taken as a sign of abdication by many protestant MPs. William and Mary wisely signed the famous 'Bill of Rights', which kept monarchs as heads of state, but permanently limited their powers. In 1690, William defeated his father-in-law James at the Battle of the Boyne, where James had gone to rally Irish Catholics. This time James II gave up; he and some family members went to live in exile in Europe. William was allowed to keep the throne when Mary died of smallpox in 1694.

TROUBLE AT TEIGNMOUTH

Today Teignmouth is a lovely seaside town where many people take holidays and would love to live. Back in 1690 though, the locals would have given anything to get out. In July of that year Teignmouth was invaded by French privateers (glorified pirates, usually with the backing of their own country), who destroyed over 100 buildings after looting them. Many people had to sleep in fields until help came from other areas. Thankfully the invasion got no further! This was the last time that mainland England (as opposed to the British Isles) was invaded by a foreign country.

THE 'NICE PIRATE'?

The late Stuart and Early Georgian eras were notorious for piracy and Devon had its share of famous ones! Henry Avery was born in Devon in 1659 and began his working life in the navy before turning to piracy – some say that he was miffed about not getting a promotion! Avery was tall and very good looking, and it is said that many wealthy women fell for his charms and showered him with gifts, which he took eagerly before loving and leaving them. A novel form of piracy! Avery was a show-off and he was particularly pleased when a play, 'The Successful Pirate', was written about him. The Jolly Roger flag was supposedly his design, though this has been disputed. Avery apparently didn't like violence, or so people were led to believe – perhaps another reason he had so many fans. In reality he was not a lovable rogue and committed many violent acts. He was also an enthusiastic slave trader and on his vessels captured Africans were treated very badly, as they were on other ships. Mystery surrounds Avery as he disappeared in the 1690s. Was he killed in a skirmish or did one of his rich lovers persuade him to give up his life of crime?

Anne (1665–1714)

King William and Queen Mary had no children and the throne passed to Mary's sister, who became Queen Anne in 1702. She married Prince George of Denmark in 1683. Anne's was a sad life. She was a very large lady and endured a lot of ill health, suffering seventeen miscarriages or stillbirths. Only one child, Prince William, survived beyond babyhood but he suffered from hydrocephalus and died shortly after his 11th birthday. Queen Anne was the last of the Stuarts.

A Fiennes Traveller

Celia Fiennes was from an aristocratic family. Her father was Colonel Nathaniel Fiennes, who seems to have been quite an indulgent parent who allowed Celia an unusual amount of freedom for those days. She was an early travel writer whose diaries described her visits to many areas of England. Independent travel was very unusual for a woman at that time and she remained resolutely single all her life in order to do her own thing without having to answer to a husband or the demands of pregnancy and motherhood. In 1698, Fiennes described her visit to Exeter, admiring its spacious streets, the beauty of the cathedral and the beautiful quality of the serge cloth produced there in large quantities. Of Plymouth she remarked on the narrow, but generally clean streets and beautiful stone houses. She also admired the city's defences.

Newcomen's New Inventions

Engineer Thomas Newcomen was born in Dartmouth in 1664. Originally he worked as an ironmonger but thanks to a change in profession one of his inventions helped to usher in the Industrial Revolution, a very important development in British and world history. And it all began in a cosy domestic setting. One day Newcomen was visiting his mother, who had put the kettle on the kitchen range to make tea. Watching steam moving the kettle lid was his inspirational moment. He went on to invent a steam-powered pump that removed water from flooded mines. Previously, flooding had been a serious and dangerous problem. Hundreds of pumping engines were built. The first one was installed in a mine near Dudley in the Midlands. Today, a working Newcomen engine can be seen near Dartmouth Tourist Information Centre.

15

THE GEORGIANS: SCIENCE, ARTS AND WAR

George I (1660–1727)

As Queen Anne had no surviving children the throne passed to George of Hanover, a cousin of Anne's. George I ruled from 1714 to 1727.

Quay and Customs

On Exeter Quay stands the elegant Grade I listed red brick custom house, which dates from 1680. Here customs officials assessed the amount of customs tariff to be paid on goods coming into the city from ships docked at the quay. A large part of customs men's jobs was catching smugglers trying to avoid paying duty! Today the building houses a visitor information centre and exhibition about the quay area history. Anyone visiting should not miss the upstairs rooms where there are ornate plaster ceilings featuring flowers, leaves and various animals including snakes! A look in one of the cupboards will reveal Georgian wallpaper. As it has been protected from the light, its design and colour can still be seen. On the wall downstairs is a large metal plaque listing many customs charges for various goods. There are many goods you would expect to see such as wood, grain and livestock but there are some that surprise and amuse modern visitors such as bales of human hair, complete carriages and chimney pots!

WHAT'S IN A NAME?

Writer Daniel Defoe began his literary career writing religious pamphlets with a very dry, earnest style. Unsurprisingly, they didn't sell very well! In 1716 Defoe left his London home to visit friends in Paignton. Yet another religious book had failed to sell and the Devon break was organised to help him overcome his disappointment. Writing could not have been further from his mind in Devon, but Defoe was suddenly seized by an idea and began furiously scribbling down an adventure story. *Robinson Crusoe* was published in 1719 and became a best-seller. The inspiration for the story's title? His hostess in Paignton had been a Miss Robinson before marriage and when she married Defoe's friend she became Mrs Crusoe!

John Lethbridge (1675–1759) of Kingskerswell hated being a wool merchant and badly neglected his work. He preferred to sit by his garden pond and imagine a life at sea, which had been his first choice of career. (His father, like many others in those days, had insisted that John had to follow him in the family business.) While idling by the pond one day in 1715 an idea struck John. He then spent several days altering a large wooden barrel, adding bellows and a window to it. He threw it into the pond and as it sank he climbed in, returning safely later. He had invented the first diving machine. This was used in salvage and made him very rich.

Lucky Lucombe

In around 1720, gardener William Lucombe founded his own plant nursery. His business flourished, but he is best known for the 'discovery', in 1762, that when turkey oaks crossbreed with cork oaks, their offspring do not lose their leaves in the winter as most oaks do. Turkey oaks are native to southern Europe. Soon the owners of large country estates all wanted a Lucombe oak or two to brighten up their gardens in winter. They also have interesting variegated bark, which is very attractive. Even better, they grow faster than other oaks, meaning that the initial owner stood a chance of seeing a mature specimen instead of leaving the privilege to descendants.

George II (1727–60)

George II was the last of our monarchs not to be born here. He has been depicted as a bit of a fool who hated reading and lacked confidence in his own abilities. He married Caroline of Ansbach in 1705. They were a devoted couple and had nine children. Unfortunately, George had a terrible relationship with his oldest son and heir, Prince Frederick.

Two Great Fires!

A huge fire in Crediton in August 1743 destroyed around 400 buildings on and near the High Street, leaving over 400 families with nowhere to live and with no belongings. The value of the destroyed homes was put at £4,000. The fire was worse than it might have been because the town's pumps didn't work: the river level was too low because there was a drought. A family escaping a fire in their house found that they were trapped by flames outside, too. Only two survived. They ran through the flames and were badly burned. Several people were killed when buildings collapsed, and firefighters also died in an accident that happened when they were trying to blow up a building to stop the fire spreading. Other fires occurred in 1763, 1766 and 1772. With fires happening so close together, arson was suspected, though no one was ever charged. Tiverton also experienced a number of fires, with particularly serious ones in 1731 and 1794.

China Finder

From an early age, William Cookworthy of Kingsbridge had to support his family after the death of his father. In spite of his wish to study art, William was forced to become an apprentice chemist. On a walking holiday in Cornwall in 1748 his knowledge of chemistry was put to good use when he found china clay (also known as kaolin, a byproduct of granite that has weathered and crumbled over millions of years). This was an important discovery as the only other source of the material was China. Soon this led to an important Cornish industry employing thousands. A boom in the manufacture of china household wares followed. China clay also became an important ingredient in medicines, which is fitting given Cookworthy's occupation as a chemist! He could have made a lot of money from his discovery, but apart from giving a lot to charity he was uninterested in wealth and instead devoted more time to his first love – art.

Coade for Success

Eleanor Coade was born in Exeter in 1733 and began her working life selling cloth household items. This would not have been an unusual occupation for a woman in the Georgian era, but a move to London changed Eleanor's life and the materials she worked with. She invented Coade 'stone' – actually a hard-wearing ceramic alternative to stone, many types of which can erode badly. Coade stone was made of glass, flint and quartz, which was mixed with clay and then fired. The material does not weather or suffer pollution damage, won't chip or shrink and is very, very hard! This means that many examples of the material can still be seen today in Devon, around Britain and further afield. Coad stone was mostly used to make statues, ornamental window and door frames and other types of building ornamentation. Its natural colour varies from white and cream to pale grey, which worked in most settings. Successful businesswomen were not common in the Georgian era. Eleanor never married, partly because her ineffectual father had ruined the family and she had seen her mother suffer because of it, and partly because a husband could legally take charge of her Coade stone business and its profits in those days. However, Eleanor did use the title 'Mrs' to lend herself an air of respectability and to ward off men!

Ask for Axminster

In 1755, cloth manufacturer Thomas Whitty of Axminster was struggling because of a slump in trade. Then he saw his first Turkish carpet and was stunned by the bright, complicated pattern and huge size. Back home, Whitty began making small carpet samples of similar designs.

These proved to be very popular, so he made a larger one. Because of the size and complicated pattern, Whitty knew the carpets would have to be very expensive. At first he worried that they wouldn't sell. Then King George II visited Axminster with his wife, Queen Charlotte. She loved Whitty's carpets so much that the King ordered one on the spot, followed by other members of the Royal family. What the Royals had, everyone else with pretentions of grandeur also had to have. Soon Whitty was teaching former weavers how to make the carpet designs and making himself a lot of money. Axminster still has a carpet manufacturer. There are still designs to suit palaces and stately homes but today many of the patterns (and plains) are made to work well in modern houses. And they last … and last!

Wrecking

The rugged coasts and rough seas of north Devon were ideal locations for a notorious activity – wrecking. This was the deliberate act of using lights to bring floundering ships too close in to shore so that they were wrecked on rocks. In many cases the lights were deliberately placed to look like markers for a safe channel. Hundreds of sailors drowned because of wrecking. There are even stories of local people murdering any sailors who managed to get to shore. This was partly to stop them claiming a share of the ship's cargo, but mostly to make sure that they couldn't complain to the authorities! People from coastal villages would flock to the beach when a ship was wrecked, gleefully collecting any cargo that floated close to the shore. At low tide the wrecked ship would be stripped of usable materials. Many houses in coastal villages had tables, doors and beams made from ships' timbers. Valuables such as navigation instruments were sold. Buyers didn't usually ask too many questions! In 1870 a law was passed offering rewards to those who rescued shipwreck victims. At Hartland Quay visitors can admire the starkly beautiful, but dangerous, coast.

GEORGE III (1760–1820)

George III was the son of the late Frederick Prince of Wales. He married Princess Charlotte of Mecklenburg-Strelitz in 1761 and had fifteen children. George III had his first bout of 'madness' in 1788. The most serious attack occurred in 1810, and permanently incapacitated him.

DARTMOOR PRISON

During the Napoleonic wars (1803–15) French prisoners were held at Plymouth in rotting old ships known as hulks. At first just a few prisoners were held but eventually there were many. Plymouth's authorities began to worry that escaped Frenchmen could swim across Plymouth Sound and attack the city. Dartmoor Prison was high on Dartmoor, so the French prisoners were sent there instead. The bleak stone walls and isolated location must have filled its prisoners with dread as they approached. The prison still operates today, though conditions for inmates have improved vastly since the days when French soldiers were badly abused, ill fed and freezing cold. American prisoners of war were also imprisoned at Dartmoor when England was at war with America in 1812.

Dartmoor Prison's old entrance

All at Sea

In 1815 Napoleon was finally defeated by the Duke of Wellington at Waterloo, which of course caused quite a lot of jubilation. People in the Torbay area had a lot more to be excited about though. Not only had the Napoleonic Wars come to an end, but a new and thrilling villain, none other than Napoleon himself, was in their midst. Well, safely imprisoned in a ship, HMS *Bellerophon* off the coast, actually. Senior British naval officers banned anyone from approaching by boat, but of course no one took a blind bit of notice. Soon anyone with a semi-seaworthy vessel was dangerously jostling for position along with up to a hundred other boats surrounding the *Bellerophon*. Boat owners did a roaring trade showing the defeated enemy taking his forlorn morning stroll around the deck. On seeing a boat approach, Napoleon would bow politely. Wealthy locals began to have a sneaking sympathy for their former enemy, who was used to better things than ship's food and cramped accommodation. Soon food and clothing were being sent to him. Worried that he had become a figure to be pitied, the ship was moved, and then Napoleon was sent into exile.

Mutiny!

Who hasn't heard of the Mutiny on the *Bounty* and the notoriously cruel Captain William Bligh? He was born in Plymouth in 1754 and served in the navy from a young age. Captain Bligh was a man of action. When the admiralty told him to take a cargo of bread fruits from New Guinea to the West Indies thousands of miles away to plant for feeding slaves there, Bligh was cross. He was a trained naval officer, not a delivery boy! It didn't help that he was given the nickname 'Bligh the Bread'. As well as being violent and bad tempered, he had no sense of humour. On the voyage to the East Indies, Bligh punished his crew savagely, taking his frustration out on them. This led to the famous mutiny when Fletcher Christian, a young lieutenant, took over the ship. Bligh was set adrift in a boat with the sailors who were still loyal to him. The mutineers reached Pitcairn Island in the South Pacific, where they settled. Their descendants still live there today. Bligh, an expert sailor, managed to navigate his way back to England. The story is familiar today because of two films. *Mutiny on the Bounty* (1935) starred Charles Laughton as Captain Bligh and Clark Gable as Fletcher Christian, and *The Bounty* (1984) starred Anthony Hopkins as Bligh and Mel Gibson as Christian.

Oh! They Did Like to be Beside the Seaside ...

In the Georgian era, wars in Europe ruined the holiday plans of many wealthy English people, who could no longer get to many European holiday destinations safely or easily. This made holidays at home more popular for the wealthy who could afford them and could take time off. Most people headed to the seaside, and Devon became particularly popular. Former tiny fishing villages began to expand with the influx of rich visitors. Exmouth is said to have been the first designated sea bathing town for visitors to Devon. Sidmouth became so popular that wealthy visitors began to have holiday 'cottages' built. In reality these were often large and well-appointed houses. Many hotels were built for visitors, too. Today, Sidmouth still has many fine examples of Georgian architecture.

In the winter of 1819 Sidmouth's most illustrious guests were Edward, Duke of Kent, son of King George III, Edward's wife,

Royal Glen Hotel, Sidmouth

Victoria of Saxe-Coburg-Saalfeld, and their baby daughter, Princess Victoria, aged 9 months. She was a particularly important infant, being directly in line to the throne as none of her older uncles had legitimate children. Sidmouth was much healthier for a small child than dirty polluted London. Her father, Edward, was also badly in debt, so the move to Sidmouth allowed him to avoid London debt collectors. The substantial Woolbrook Cottage was rented for them and the family planned to stay for a long time. Sadly this was not to be. While walking on the beach one blustery sleety day Edward caught a chill. Instead of staying in the warm, tough Edward insisted on going out the following day. The chill turned to pneumonia and he died. The cottage they stayed in is now the Royal Glen Hotel.

The Rise of Exmouth

Lady Francis Nelson had a sad life. Orphaned at an early age, she was widowed early too when her first husband, a doctor, died. She married Horatio Nelson in 1787 and was content to look after her husband's infirm father while Nelson was away making a name for himself with his naval exploits. Nelson, who was admired by many women, became bored with Francis. He began an affair with Lady Emma Hamilton and had a daughter, Horatia, with her. Lady Francis was a huge source of gossip among her acquaintances. To escape it she moved to Exmouth, then a small, quiet fishing and boat-building town. Francis lived at number 6 The Beacon, a fine terraced house with a sea view. Soon other wealthy people followed, having holiday homes built or renting suites in one of the new luxury hotels. Francis was partly responsible for the rise in Exmouth's tourist trade.

Rogue Religion

In the 1760s a young woman named Joanna Southcott of Gittisham left home to become a maid. Her own family had been quite well off, but her father was very lazy and careless with his business and he lost most of his money. Her new lowly status annoyed Joanna. When her wealthier London relatives refused to help she was livid. Her Methodist family carefully placed Joanna with a respectable Methodist minister and his family but Joanna was soon fed up with her new job. She also grew bored with having to attend so many church services and listen to religious discussions carried out by visiting Methodists at her employer's home. In 1792, possibly for fun, she began to pretend to have 'religious experiences' with 'shaking' and 'visions'. Most people were scornful, but over the years some were taken in and gave money, which she said would be given to good causes. Instead it went into her own pocket. This wasn't enough for greedy Joanna, who left her job and began to write and sell leaflets and books about her 'experiences'. This went on for years and she became quite rich. Then, aged over 60, she claimed to be pregnant and expecting the new Messiah. Money and gifts flooded in, but of course no child was born. Accused of fraud and threatened with imprisonment, Joanna apparently fell into a trance and died a few days later, probably from a stroke. She was buried in London. A few days after her funeral her gravestone suddenly shattered. This was due to it being hit by stray bullets from nearby army manoeuvres. Her followers, though, were convinced that God had destroyed the stone from anger at the way his 'disciple' had been treated. It is strange how many people were taken in, but even stranger that a small cult of 'Joanna' believers still exists today!

PLAYWRIGHTS FOR WOMEN!

Playwright Hannah Cowley was born above her father's bookshop in Tiverton in 1743. Hannah was a keen reader from an early age and, like her mother, was an advocate for improvements in women's rights. Unusually for those days, Hannah was encouraged by both parents to take education seriously and they were proud of her efforts to become a writer. After her marriage, Hannah moved to London with her husband and was keen to go to theatres. However, in those days many respectable women felt they were not suitable places for them to visit. Hannah decided to change all that by becoming a playwright herself. Her plays have a feminist theme on the subjects of forced marriage, lack of rights for women and horrible husbands! Her best-known plays include *The Belle's Stratagem* and *Who's the Dupe?* The building where Hannah was brought up is now a café called The Coffee Bean.

WILLIAM IV 1830–37

William IV never expected to be king and had made a career in the Royal Navy. He was nearly 70 when he came to the throne.

DON'T RAT ON JACK!

Jack Rattenbury, from Beer, was born in the 1770s. He was Devon's most famous and infamous smuggler. Jack's father died, leaving a large, very young impoverished family. As the eldest, Jack went to sea on fishing boats for a few pennies while still a child. But this didn't bring in enough to support his family. Before he reached his teens, Jack had hit upon a more lucrative job – smuggling! Soon he had his own boat that, he claimed, was found adrift, but was most likely stolen.

During a long career, Jack was shot at by customs officers and regularly had to throw himself off his boat and swim under water to avoid capture. No one ever turned Jack in because his ill-gotten gains were used to help many poor families. If Jack's boat was confiscated by customs men he somehow always got it back. Even the local vicar turned a blind eye and would vouch untruthfully for his whereabouts whenever customs men asked questions. If customs men happened to be prowling near the church, a lady dressed in black would stand near the vault crying into a handkerchief and the officers would discreetly slip away without making a search. Beer caves were another handy hiding place. Local women often volunteered to flirtatiously distract customs officials so that Jack could make his escape, and on a number of occasions he hid inside a hollow wall in the local pub to evade capture. Whenever Jack went in for a drink, there would be lookouts stationed nearby to warn him of approaching customs men. It seems that they were easily fooled. Several times when customs men landed and got too near to Jack, their boat mysteriously broke its moorings, causing the officials to rush off to retrieve it. Perhaps some of the customs men had a sneaking respect for Jack?

In 1832 Jack, who was illiterate, related his smuggling exploits to a writer, who produced a book called *Memoirs of a Smuggler.* Lots of copies were made and circulated. Jack was not arrested after admitting his crimes – by this time he was getting old and arthritic and had given up smuggling. Also, the authorities were worried that if they prosecuted Jack, his supporters would cause trouble. Smuggling in Devon continued into the 1850s, but the Georgian era and Jack were its heyday.

CHOLERA!

In 1832, like many other areas, Devon was hit by a particularly bad cholera epidemic. The disease probably came from the Far East along trade routes and entered England through a north-eastern port, from where it spread to other areas. Many towns were affected, including Exeter, Plymouth, Dartmouth and Bideford. The disease made its way inland, affecting many other areas, too. Symptoms of cholera included severe diarrhoea, terrible stomach and limb cramps, and dehydration causing organ failure. Doctors were powerless to help. Today we know that cholera is spread by a bacterium and is caught by drinking contaminated water. As in most towns in 1832, most Devon water supplies were dirty! In those days, however, most people, including doctors, believed that cholera was caught by breathing in contaminated air. The frightening speed of death from cholera can be seen from the experience of one unfortunate Plymouth woman, who in July 1832 had spent the morning doing laundry, baking and drinking tea with a neighbour. At 4 p.m. she began to experience stomach pains, diarrhoea and sickness. A doctor was called at 6 p.m. and she died in agony at 7.30 p.m. Over 1,000 Plymouth people also died of the disease.

Like many towns during a cholera outbreak, those in Devon began hurried clean-ups, with mass street swillings and throwing down of lime, but it was too little too late. Exeter's cholera outbreak is the best documented thanks to Doctor Thomas Shapter, who later wrote a book about his experiences, *The History of Cholera in Exeter in 1832*. Shapter's book contained a map showing the location of each cholera death and it was noted that the disease was more prevalent in poor, dirty, overcrowded areas. In Exeter, graveyards filled up and Bury Meadow on the city outskirts was turned into a burial site. There were many claims that people were buried before they were dead in an unsuccessful attempt to halt the disease.

Bury Meadow was not given this name because of cholera burials. Its history goes back many years earlier when the site was a field owned by a Mr Berry. 'Bury' is a corruption of his name. Today Bury Meadow is a pleasant park.

As cholera came along the south coast in 1832 the people of Exeter waited fretfully for it to strike. Then a miracle seemed to have happened. Cholera slipped over the

Exe Estuary and made its way to Plymouth. Exeter folk breathed a collective sigh of relief. Church services and bell ringing were organised to give thanks, but to no avail. An Exeter lady who had been visiting friends in Plymouth unwittingly brought cholera back with her!

Water Rotten Job

In Exeter before modern water systems were built, the city employed water carriers to deliver to homes. They drove their horses and carts into shallow parts of the River Exe and scooped the water into barrels. The job was very badly paid and hard work. Most of the people employed in this were very poor, often sick or crippled and unable to find another occupation. On several occasions altercations between the water carriers and unsympathetic youths meant that the police had to be fetched. The youths would pull the bungs out of the water carrier's barrels while they were walking up paths making deliveries.

16

VICTORIAN AND EDWARDIAN INNOVATION AND MORE EXPLORATION

VICTORIA (1837–1901)

Victoria only came to the throne because her late father's older brothers had no legitimate children. She was only 18 when she became Queen. In the Victorian Age Britain's colonial holdings grew and technology advanced.

EDWARD VII (1901–10)

Unfortunately Edward VII could never live up to his father's expectations. He became the original party prince and was infamous for the number of lovers he had!

WAR LEADERS

LT COLONEL WILLIAM MORRIS

The Crimean War was was fought by Britain, France and Turkey against Russia because Russian expansionism threatened the West. Lt Colonel William Morris of Devon took part in the doomed Charge of the Light Brigade when British troops were ordered to charge directly into Russian guns.

Colonel John Rouse Chard VC

In 1879 the Zulu War broke out in Africa. British forces met strong resistance from the Zulus; the most famous battle was Rorkes Drift where a tiny British force commanded by John Chard from Plymouth defeated a huge Zulu army.

General Sir Redvers Buller VC

Buller was British Commander-in-Chief in the Boer war which was fought between Britain and South Africa and the Orange Free State from 1899 to 1902. The war was about control of gold mining. Many Devon soldiers were involved and Buller was brought out of retirement to lead the army. The British triumphed but he was made to resign for some of his decisions. However, Buller was popular with his troops. A statue of him on his horse can be found in North Road, Exeter, partly paid for by his men. Buller lived at his family estate Downes House near Crediton.

WANDERLUST AND EXPLORATION

ON THE ORIGIN OF SPECIES

In 1831 a ship with a soon-to-be very influential crew member sailed from Plymouth on a five-year voyage. The ship was HMS *Beagle* and the passenger was Charles Darwin (1809–82), who was just 22 years old and employed as the ship's naturalist. He collected animal and plant specimens whenever the *Beagle* landed. While studying the variations found in the same species on different Galapagos islands, Darwin formulated his famous Theory of Evolution, which is laid out in his ground-breaking book *On the Origin of Species*, published in 1859. This proved that animals developed and changed to suit their environment, with the best adapted surviving to reproduce. To begin with his ideas created scandal and argument as a lot of people, especially churchmen, felt that Darwin was denying God's influence and power. In many circles Darwin became very unpopular, but within a few years his evolutionary theories became accepted by all but a few religious fundamentalist groups.

NILE BE SEEING YOU

Explorer Richard Francis Burton was born in Torquay in 1821 and his colleague, John Hanning Speke, was born in Buckland Brewer in 1827. Both were rebels who had very liberal upbringings – Burton was thrown out of Oxford University – and they were constantly in trouble with senior officers during their army careers. In 1856 the Royal Geographical Society commissioned them to find the source of the River Nile in Africa. They reached Lake Tanganyika in 1858, at first mistaking it as the source. Further travels finally proved that Lake Victoria (named by them after the

Queen) was the actual source. Fame and fortune followed their discoveries. Unfortunately both men fell ill with various African diseases for which they had no immunity, and Speke's health was permanently impaired.

Richard Francis Burton spoke thirty-five languages, many learned during his time in the subcontinent of India. He translated many books from Indian languages to English. The most controversial of these was the Kama Sutra. His wife burned his copy!

Awful Antarctic

Captain Robert Falcon Scott was born in Devonport in 1868 and attended HMS Britannia Naval College. Scott proved to be a very good naval officer and was a gifted scientist. In 1900 he commanded the National Arctic Expedition and was noted for his concern for his men in the hazardous Antarctic conditions. He returned to England and took up the command of various vessels. However, Scott had got the exploration bug and was keen to get back to Antarctica in spite of its perils. In 1910, Scott and his team set off for a race with Norwegian Roald Amundsen to be the first to reach the South Pole. Unfortunately when Scott's party got there they found a Norwegian flag – Amundsen had beaten them to it! The team were utterly dismayed but worse was to come. On their return journey to the coast and their ship, the weather became severe, with howling winds and blizzards hampering their progress. Soon the men's frostbite began to turn gangrenous. Their starved bodies were found in their tent by a search party in 1912.

Captain Oates, who was the first to become very sick, sacrificed himself in the hope that the rest of the team could go faster without him and get back to their ship. Leaving the tent, Oates uttered the now legendary words, 'I am just going outside and I may be some time.'

Vile Vicars and a Satanist

Sour Grapes

John Froud became the vicar of St Peter's Church in the early 1800s after leaving university. As he had been courting for some time he fully expected his lady love to accept his proposal and join him in his rural parish. Alas! She wanted more than a poor vicar could provide and said no. Froude became a terrible vicar; he could barely be bothered to conduct services, appeared drunk at funerals and ignored all social invitations from the gentry in the area. Perhaps Froud was depressed, but this doesn't explain why he took up with a band of ne'er do wells who enjoyed boozing, chasing 'loose' women and wilfully damaging property. In spite of all this, Froud surprisingly remained vicar of St Peter's for nearly fifty years.

Hooray Henry!

Quite possibly Henry Philpotts was the most unpopular of Exeter's seventy-one bishops. During his tenure, which lasted from 1831 to 1868, he was disliked by Exeter Cathedral staff because he was bad-tempered, rude and vindictive. The people of Exeter found him snobbish, unapproachable and unsympathetic when they had problems. Most people managed to maintain their manners when Philpotts was rude to them but he had to be rescued on the street by the police on more than one occasion when he got into fisticuffs with less respectful people. On top of this, the bishop spent far too much time at his grand mansion in Torquay. So how did Philpotts manage to remain bishop for so long? Perhaps having a powerful and wealthy family helped.

Murderous!

The mid-Devon Village of Lapford has a very pretty and peacefully located church, but in the 1860s a horrible event took place that rocked the village to the core. The new curate was found horribly murdered in the churchyard. The young man had been seen winking at Vicar Radford's pretty young wife, much to the fury of her husband. Two and two were soon put together and Radford was found guilty of the terrible crime. Fortunately for him the jury refused to sentence him. As one said, 'We ain't never 'ung a vicar yet an' we ain't goin' to start now!' Amazingly, Radford made up with his wife and was allowed to keep his job.

Devon Dog and Dog Collar

Parson Jack Russell, who was vicar of St James Church, Swimbridge, was educated at Oxford University and came from a good family. He was not a favourite of his bosses, Bishops Henry Phillpotts and Frederick Temple, though. They were unimpressed by Jack's hard drinking and the amount of time he devoted to hunting instead of carrying out his religious duties. But Jack was popular with his flock as many of them were hunting, shooting and fishing types, too. He was the vicar of St James for over forty years from 1841. He is well known for his capacity for having a good time and even better known for developing the Jack Russell breed of dogs. Parson Russell needed a hunting dog that was easy to train, small enough to get down animal burrows and was keen on hunting, but friendly with humans. Today, sturdy Jack Russells with their short white coats and either brown or black patches are popular all over the world. The human Jack Russell was sturdy himself and, much to the annoyance of church authorities, continued hunting enthusiastically until just before he died aged 88 in 1883.

WICKEDEST!

Aleister Crowley, the infamous occultist who was known as 'the 'Wickedest Man in the World', was born in 1875. He lived in Barton, a suburb of respectable Torquay, for part of his life. Crowley was born into a Plymouth Brethren family, in those days a branch of fundamentalist Christianity who were brought up to beware sin and sinfulness. He rejected his family religion from an early age, fed up with being punished for refusing to conform. After his father's early death, Crowley became obsessed with sadomasochistic sex, drink and drugs. After a row about his behaviour, his mother called him a 'beast' and he gleefully adopted the nickname 'Beast 666', i.e. the Devil. Many people began to refer to him as the Anti-Christ.

Crowley began a new religion known as Thelema, which urged its followers to abandon established morals and behaviour and instead adopt the idea that they could do anything they wanted. It was inspired by the ancient Egyptian God Horus, the 'Distant One', who was a vengeful protector of the upper classes. Horus' story is shrouded in mystery and mysticism with a hint of cruelty, and Crowley identified with him and adopted Middle Eastern clothing and eating habits, both of which fascinated his detractors in spite of themselves. In spite of his growing reputation for evil beliefs, he married Rose Kelley, who was from a very conventional background. She soon strayed from the straight and narrow and it was rumoured that she actually taught her husband how to summon up evil spirits! Dabbling in the occult eventually had a very bad effect on Rose, who developed serious mental health issues. When Crowley died in 1947 his followers hijacked his funeral and turned it into a pagan ceremony, to the horror of the few conventional people who attended. Today he is seen as a slightly sinister but comical figure by most people, though he still manages to outrage some. An exhibition about Crowley, complete with a recording of his sinister voice, can be seen at the Witchcraft Museum in Boscastle, Cornwall.

INDUSTRY

ISAMBARD KINGDOM BRUNEL IN DEVON
OH RATS!

In 1844 there was much excitement in Exeter because the first train arrived to cheering, flag-waving crowds. In 1849 the railway ran through Newton Abbot as far as Plymouth. Its senior engineer was Isambard Kingdom Brunel. He was born in 1806 and was the most famous engineer of his day. His ship, the SS *Great Britain*, was the biggest ever at that time, and he built bridges spanning long distances, including the Saltash Bridge over the Tamar near Plymouth. He also constructed the first tunnel under the Thames.

In Devon Brunel is best known for the Great Western Railway that took passengers from London to the West. Brunel was a genius, but he sometimes got it wrong! He insisted on using a 7ft-wide railway line, which caused problems when this joined systems with narrower gauges. The railway line from Exeter to Plymouth was a disaster because he adopted the Atmospheric System, which was powered by air running through pipes on the tracks. The air then moved piston rods and propelled the train. Pumping stations along the track were able to open or close leather flaps along the route to regulate the air flow. Brunel thought he could save money with the system and, had it worked, it would have been very green, though there was little concern about environmental issues in those days. Unfortunately the system failed because rats kept eating the leather flaps, which had to be replaced at great expense! One of Brunel's pumping stations can still be seen at Starcross. As the railway line runs past Dawlish, two unusual rock formations can be seen in the sea. Known as the Parson and the Clerk, legend says that they were two churchmen turned to stone by the Devil! Other railway lines to open in Devon included Exeter to Crediton and Exeter to Exmouth.

Railway pumping station, Starcross

Hail the Huge

In 1854 Brunel built the Royal Albert Bridge across the River Tamar, linking the railways of south Devon and Cornwall. It is a remarkable structure over 1,400ft long with three spans, which were more recently partly repaired or strengthened. The granite foundations of the bridge are in deep water and the fact that they managed to get them in place with the equipment they had in those days is a miracle in itself. To allow men to work at the bottom of the foundation in relative safety, a huge tube was sunk with its top above the level of the river water. The bridge was opened by Prince Albert himself.

Much Ado at Morwellam Quay

In the 900s on the border between Devon and Cornwall the Monks at Tavistock began to use Morwellam as a means to transport produce and other goods down to boats by packhorse. West Devon developed a huge and lucrative mining industry, and tin, copper arsenic and manganese was transported from Morwellam. Eventually a canal was built, making transportation to Morwellam easier. In the Georgian era a huge deposit of copper was discovered near Morwellam and a mine was begun. This was named the George and Charlotte Mine after King George III and Queen Charlotte.

Today, visitors to Morwellam Quay can take a trip into the mine and learn about the hard life of a miner. In the Victorian era an even larger copper vein (one of the biggest in the world) was opened and a new quay was built. Many people with money in mining became very rich, but not the miners themselves. Morwellam Quay became a community with homes for the miners, other workers and their families, a public house and even a school. Morwellam's prosperity was not to last, though. Eventually railways proved to be a much faster, cheaper and more convenient way to transport goods and Morwellam, once an important mine, closed. Today it has become a fascinating 'living' museum. As well as a mine, trip visitors can see miners' houses, a giant waterwheel that was once Morwellam's power source, a renovated ore crushing machine, restored docks and even a ship! Staff dress and act the parts of Victorian miners, sailors, their wives and children. This can be a bit disconcerting for visitors. And the best way to deal with this is to join in the dressing up yourself!

Victoria to the Rescue!

When the lace-making machine was invented it looked like the end for Honiton lace makers. Machine lace was much cheaper and soon almost anyone could afford a bit to adorn a special outfit. Wealthy people promptly stopped having lots of lace on their garments. Hearing of the plight of destitute lace makers, Queen Victoria decided to help. She was planning her wedding to Prince Albert and ordered a wedding dress, veil, underskirts and corset covers made entirely of handmade lace from Honiton. Suddenly, handmade lace was fashionable again, at least while Victoria was Queen. Tourists marvelled at the deft workers, who made elaborate floral patterns using pins stuck into pillows to form a frame to weave the lace. So complex were the patterns that often 300 pins were used in one small piece. People gave lengths of it as presents and Honiton lace found its way to other countries. Often the lace was detachable and passed down the generations. Victoria's intervention caused a temporary boom in the handmade lace industry, and at this time Devon lace was superior to that of other countries.

Working and living conditions for lace makers had always been bad and many went blind because of the close work in ill-lit cottages. Children were employed from the age of 4 because of their nimble fingers. They often worked twelve hours a day or more and were sickly from a lack of fresh air. Changing fashions sent the lace-making industry into another slump in the 1870s. This was made worse by the Education Act of 1880, which made education compulsory from age 5 to 12, although at least this stopped child labour. Today, lace-making classes run in several Devon locations, but handmade lace is now really only a craft hobby.

Plymouth Pepper Pot

Anyone who has been to Plymouth Hoe will be familiar with Smeaton's Tower, the red and white pepper pot-shaped structure. This is part of a lighthouse that was once located on Eddystone Rocks, several miles off Plymouth, to warn ships away. Smeaton's was the third lighthouse there. The stories of the first two are filled with disaster. Number one and its builder were washed away in a storm. Number two was made of wood and the lantern burnt it down. Smeaton's Lighthouse lasted for a hundred years but was eventually replaced. Today, the Douglas Lighthouse, which was built in 1882, stands on Eddystone Rocks. A song about Smeaton's lighthouse was written in 1850 and is still popular at folk music events.

The Keeper of the Eddystone Light

Oh, me father was the keeper of the Eddystone light,
And he slept with a mermaid one fine night,
From this union there came three,
A porpoise and a porgy and the other was me.

Chorus:
Yo ho,
The wind blows free,
Oh for the life on the rolling sea.

One day as I was a-trimmin' the glim,
Humming a tune from the evening hymn,
A voice from the starboard shouted, 'Ahoy',
And there was me mother a-sittin' on the buoy.

Chorus

Oh what has become of me children three?
Me mother then she asked of me,
One was exhibited as a talking fish,
The other was served in a chafing dish.

Chorus

Then the phosphorus flashed in her seaweed hair,
I looked again, but me mother wasn't there,
But I heard her voice echoing back through the night,
The devil take the keeper of the Eddystone light!

All Write in Devon

Elizabeth Barrett Browning (1806–61) lived in Torquay from 1838. She had lung disease and the mild climate suited her. Although ill she wrote many poems such as 'How Do I Love Thee?' and 'The Seraphim'.

Charles Dickens (1812–75) spent a lot of time in Exeter as a young reporter. Later he moved his parents from London to Alphington, Exeter, as it was cheaper than London. His more famous works include *A Christmas Carol* and *Great Expectations*.

Charles Kingsley (1819–75) wrote his most famous novel, *Westward Ho!*, about Tudor seafarers. This was inspired by the little fishing villages in Devon with their narrow streets where smugglers hid goods. Other works by Kingsley include *The Water Babies*.

R.D. Blackmore (1825–1900) was educated at Blundell's School, Tiverton. He became a lawyer in 1852, but dabbled in writing. In 1869 he wrote his most famous novel, *Lorna Doone*. Set on Exmoor, the story has romance, feuds, murder and rebellion.

Rev Sabine Baring Gould (1834–1924) wrote hundreds of folklore books, religious pamphlets and hymns, and wrote down traditional songs to preserve them. But he also had a play and a film written about him and his wife. The Play was *Pygmalion*, which was turned into the film *My Fair Lady*, made in 1964. In it a poor flower seller is educated and taught polite manners. Baring Gould, vicar and landowner of Lew Trenchard, married a mill worker and educated her himself.

Arthur Conan Doyle (1859–1930) is the author of the Sherlock Holmes stories. The most famous of these is *The Hound of the Baskervilles*, set on Dartmoor. Conan Doyle was inspired by a story about an evil, violent man named

Richard Cabel who lived on Dartmoor in the 1600s. When Cabel died, a pack of vicious, black wild dogs came to his grave every night howling and pawing the ground. They were known as the 'devil dogs', said to be out to claim the Devil's own.

The Royal Albert Memorial Museum

In 1868 this newly built museum (known as the RAMM) was dedicated to Prince Albert, Queen Victoria's late husband. He was an intellectual who had lent his support to many educational venues and had sadly died aged only 42 in 1861.The RAMM had free reading rooms and displays of artefacts that fascinated Victorian people who, of course, had few other ways to see such intriguing items. As well as the general public, the museum attracted some of the major intellectuals in the country and was important in the later development of the University of Exeter.

In 2007, RAMM underwent major improvements including a large extension, and it opened again in 2011. A thoroughly modern museum, today it is inviting yet informative and has something to interest every visitor. Children particularly love the widescreen film about early Devon, complete with dinosaurs, or dressing up as Roman soldiers. Displays of prehistoric and historic artefacts are informative yet fun. Other displays include costumes from around the world, art, Egyptology, pottery (the astonishing medieval puzzle jug is a must see), insects and stuffed animals from around the world. Visitors literally can't miss Gerald the Giraffe, whose incredible height means that he takes up space on two floors! More recently, the museum has acquired the Seaton Down Hoard, a fascinating collection of over 20,000 Roman coins found by someone using a metal detector!

THE THEATRE ROYAL FIRE

The people of Victorian Exeter had very bad luck with their theatres as three of them burnt down! The first was the Bedford Circus theatre in 1820, although thankfully no one was killed. A few years later the same fate befell another theatre and again there were no casualties. In 1887 the Grand Theatre Royal opened at the top of Longbrook Street in the city. One evening, the audience was watching a performance of 'Rominy Rye', a play about a young man who chose to live and work with gypsies because he was bored of his studies. The performance was going well as the curtain closed for the end of the first half. Then disaster struck! The stage curtain caught fire and this was fed by the gas used in lighting. Soon the whole place was an inferno and 167 people were killed, either by smoke inhalation or being burnt to death. At an inquest it was discovered that emergency exits were too few and too narrow, the curtain had not been made of flameproof material and fire hoses were not working properly. Worse still, the theatre could have had electricity, which would have been safer than gas, but it was not installed because it was more expensive. Rescuers and those who had to retrieve bodies spoke of having to remove charred remains. Some could not be identified and families had to assume that their missing loved ones were among them.

In 1889, a new Theatre Royal was built on the same site. This time stringent fire precautions were taken that were also adopted by other theatres in Britain and other countries. This theatre lasted until the 1960s, first as a live performance venue and later as a cinema. Today, a modern office block stands on the site. A man who once worked as a young projectionist at the Theatre Royal has claimed that he and his co-workers once heard the ghostly screams and running feet of the victims of the earlier fire.

Fairs

Tavistock Goosey Fair

The lively and humorously named Goosey Fair has taken place every year since 1823, but probably goes back to the 1200s. The fair is on the second Wednesday of October. There used to be thousands of geese for sale and people would buy one each year to fatten up for Christmas dinner. Sadly, live geese no longer put in an appearance in any quantity due to laws to stop the spread of disease. The fair is still popular, though, with thousands of people visiting (they now outnumber the geese). Tavistock Goosey Fair is typically Devon but more and more traders come from elsewhere in Britain. Today there are roundabouts, falconry displays, face painting, children's entertainment, music, dancing and food stalls of all kinds, including goose dinners!

Widecombe Fair

An annual agricultural fair has taken place in the Dartmoor village of Widecombe since at least the 1850s. Almost certainly it had already been held for many years before this time, but on a smaller scale. Its isolated location could have been enough to keep it out of the county's news. There is a very famous traditional folk song called 'Widecombe Fair' about a Spreyton character called Tom Cobley and his efforts to get to the event. It is included here because the author has heard it sung all over Britain and in several other countries. The song 'Widecombe Fair' was first collected and published by the Rev Sabine Baring Gould in 1892. It is almost certainly much older though. Baring Gould collected and wrote down thousands of traditional songs in the Victorian era. Many of the singers were unable to write and Baring Gould wanted to preserve their songs.

Widecombe Fair Song (early nineteenth century).

Tom Pearce, Tom Pearce, lend me your grey mare,
All along, down along, out along lee,
For I want to go down to Widecombe Fair.

Chorus:
Wi' Bill Brewer, Jan Stewer, Peter Gurney,
Peter Davy, Dan'l Whiddon, Harry Hawk,
Old Uncle Tom Cobley and all,
Old Uncle Tom Cobley and all.

And when shall I see again my old grey mare?
All along, down along, out along lee,
By Friday soon or Saturday noon.

Chorus

So they harnessed and bridled the old grey mare,
All along, down along, out along, lee,
And off they drove to Widecombe fair.

Chorus

Then Friday came and Saturday soon,
All along, down along, out along lee,
Tom Pearce's old mare hath not trotted home.

Chorus

So Tom Pearce he got up to the top of the hill,
All along, down along, out along lee,
And he sees his old mare a-making her will.

Chorus

Tom Pearce's old mare, her took sick and died,
All along, down along, out along lee,
And Tom he sat down on a stone and he cried.

Chorus

But this isn't the end of this shocking affair,
All along, down along, out along lee,
Nor though they be dead, of the horrid career.

Chorus

When the wind whistles cold on the moor of a night,
All along, down along, out along lee,
Tom Pearce's old mare doth appear ghastly white.

Chorus

And all the long night be heard skirling and groans,
All along, down along, out along lee,
From Tom Pearce's old mare and her rattling bones.

Chorus

There were several generations of Cobleys in Spreyton and quite a few were called Tom! The grave of the man in the song cannot now be located. The Tom Cobley Tavern at Spreyton has lots of information about its most famous son.

17

THE FIRST WORLD WAR: TRAGEDY AND HEROISM

GEORGE V (1910–36)

George V was a second son who took the throne as his older brother died young. In the First World War he changed the family name from Saxe-Coburg-Gotha, which came from his German ancestors, to Windsor.

THE WAR BEGINS

Tales of unrest on the Continent seemed a long way away to many people. Then things got serious. Archduke Franz Ferdinand of Austria was assassinated in Sarajevo, Bosnia and Herzegovina, by revolutionary Gavrilo Princip, a Serbian nationalist. This affected many European alliances. Austria declared war on Serbia, then Germany declared war on Russia, France and Belgium. Britain declared war on Germany and its allies because of its treaties with France and Belgium.

Land Battles Involving Devon Men in the First World War

The Devon Regiment

The Devonshire Regiment was first formed in 1685 to combat the Monmouth Rebellion. Many of the new soldiers were farm labourers armed with pitchforks and axes. Unsurprisingly, the Monmouth Rebellion failed, but King James II and his advisors decided to form a properly trained Devonshire Regiment.

By the start of the First World War the Devonshire Regiment had three battalions, one in reserve. There were around 800 soldiers in a battalion. With the outbreak of war, the number expanded to twenty-five. Their most famous battle was Ypres, where they helped defend their front line and the town of Ypres. The battalions also served in France, where their most famous battle was the Somme in 1916. This was meant to push the Germans right back to Germany but the campaign failed due to bad leadership from behind the lines. In 1917, Devon regiments fought in the Battle of Passchendaele. Later some of the regiments served in Italy, Mesopotamia (now Iraq), Egypt, and Turkey.

Bravery

An officer in the Devons told of the reputation for bravery that the regiment acquired. He described how his men were frequently in the thick of the fighting, which often lasted for hours both day and night, leaving many dead or dying and the trench a mass of body parts and blood. But in each battle his fine boys managed to repel the enemy, leaving thousands of them dead. A French soldier rescued from a shell hole by two Devons told them that a captured

German had said that they were very scared of the Devons because they were so brave in battle and brilliant shots. By the end of the war the Devons had become famous throughout the army, and their relatives and the people of Devon were justified in their pride in their 'lads'. Sadly, their bravery came at a high cost. Over 6,000 Devonshire Regiment soldiers were killed in the war and 18,000 were injured, many of them seriously.

THE CHRISTMAS TRUCE 1914

Many people, including the enthusiastic recruits, expected the war to be over by Christmas 1914. Instead thousands of soldiers were still in the trenches, which were partly flooded due to the appalling weather. They were cold, wet, covered in mud and missing their families and homes. Then, on Christmas Day, something remarkable happened on a number of areas of the battle front. A Devonshire Regiment soldier recalled:

> We ate so much pudding! On Christmas Eve we managed to communicate with the Germans in the trenches in front of ours and agreed that no one would fire on Christmas Day. When it arrived we all walked about in no man's land with the enemy! Then we gave each other presents. One German gave me some tinned fruit and I gave him some writing paper. He was pleased with it as it had a nice pattern on it that his little girl, aged 6, would like. He showed me her picture – a pretty child. This touched me a lot, especially as we would soon be trying to kill each other again. Many soldiers from both sides took photographs of each other. This could have got us into trouble as we were not supposed to have cameras with us let alone take pictures of the enemy! We then played football with the Germans. They won! In the evening

we sang carols together with each side taking turns to sing. We could hear other groups doing the same in the distance. Nothing about this war made sense anymore.

NAVAL AND CIVILIAN SHIPPING

At the start of the war, Devonport Dockyard doubled its workforce to 20,000 and continued operating twenty-four hours a day. Work to construct naval vessels was always dangerous but became more so in the flurry to get more into the water. The coast of south Devon was a hunting ground for U-boats, and dozens of British ships both naval and civilian were sunk in the area. In 1914, so many of Brixham's fishermen had joined the navy that older sailors and boys were recruited to man the fishing fleet. HMS *Amphion* became the first Royal Navy vessel to be mined and sunk in the First World War in August 1914. The ship was based in Plymouth and many of its crew were from the city. On 1 November 1914, after a brave fight, British ships lost a battle off the coast of Coronel, Chile. On New Year's Day 1915, the battleship HMS *Formidable* was sunk off west Devon. Nearly 600 sailors drowned. On 3 April 1915, the British steamer *Lockwood* was torpedoed and sank. On 20 March 1917, the British naval hospital ship *Asturias* was torpedoed near Salcombe. Horrifyingly, and not for the only time, the enemy knew that their target included wounded men. Many north Devon fishing vessels were fired on by German submarines. A number were sunk, but other vessels managed to save many of the sailors. The Germans didn't get their own way off Devon though; throughout the war a number of U-boats were destroyed by the British.

Charles Lacey died in May 1915 aged 100. He was the oldest former Royal Navy veteran. Mr Lacey had served on HMS *Bellerophon*, a vessel used in 1815 – the year of Mr Lacey's birth – to hold defeated Napoleon at Torbay.

JUTLAND 1916

The naval battle of Jutland took place off the Jutland peninsula in Denmark on 31 June 1916. It was the largest sea battle by far in the First World War. Over 6,000 British seamen were killed; many of them were from the Plymouth area and some were just 15 years old. The navy lost fourteen ships, five of which came from Plymouth. Both the British and the Germans claimed tenuous victories. The outcome of the battle was seen as indecisive by many naval experts. Today, many people claim a victory for Britain because the German surface fleet was compromised after the battle because of a British blockade of German ports. The leadership of Admiral John Jellicoe and Vice Admiral David Beatty was called into question and it was felt by many that they contributed to the indecisiveness of the battle.

DEVON WOMEN IN THE FIRST WORLD WAR

DAME AGNES WESTON

Agnes Weston lived in Plymouth and came from a wealthy and religious background. Like many women of her class, she was involved in charitable work. She was particularly concerned by the plight of sailors who docked in Plymouth. Many were young and hundreds of miles from home. Sailors' lodgings were dirty and overcrowded, and lacked entertainment, so many went to pubs and drank excessively. Agnes began to badger local hospitals to provide health care for sailors. She set up hostels, known as Sailors' Rests, where they could stay cheaply, eat good food and have baths. Sailors' Rests had books, stationery and stamps for sailors to use to write to their families. There were few rules, one being that alcohol was not allowed! At first local people laughed – whoever heard of teetotal sailors? Soon though hostels were full of sober seamen, which pleased senior naval officers. Agnes worried about her 'regulars' when they were out at sea facing possible U-boat attacks. They felt able to confess their fears to her and she spent many evenings listening to them. In 1918 she was made a dame. She died just before the end of the war.

Georgiana Buller

Georgiana Buller (1884–1953) was the only child of General Sir Redvers Buller of Downes House, Crediton. Like many military men who spent a lot of time abroad with the army, General Buller married late. He and his wife adored Georgiana but brought her up to have the same sense of duty that they had. They also expected her to do something with her life instead of merely being a privileged young lady. During the First World War, Georgiana became a director of the Voluntary Aid Organisation, running hospitals for wounded troops in Exeter. The first opened in 1914. The wounded arrived at Exeter Queen Street Station (now Central Station) to loud cheers from the waiting crowd. Over four years of war, thousands of soldiers were treated. Georgiana was not medically qualified but her strength of character and illustrious background enabled her to get things done in spite of military officials who thought that she should stay at home and knit socks for the soldiers! Georgiana was compassionate to patients and their families but could get annoyed when her plans for helping the wounded were thwarted by military red tape. King George V and Queen Mary visited Exeter in 1915 to see the new military hospitals, talk with patients and congratulate the staff on their work.

After the war Georgiana was made Dame Commander of the Order of the British Empire for her war work. This would have pleased her much decorated father but he had died in 1908.

MILITARY HOSPITALS

At the start of the war, hospital supply depots were opened in Exeter and Plymouth by Lady Gertrude Hall, who managed the enterprises with a loyal assistant. Each depot had a sewing room for bandage making, a separate room for making swabs, and rooms where other medical supplies were stored. A carefully run stock assessment ensured that there were always ample supplies. Soon other women began to hunt for useful hospital items. In just a few weeks the Mayoress of Plymouth sourced 575 blankets.

By 1915 there were four main Voluntary Aid Detachment (VAD) hospitals in Exeter and one in Torbay. Very soon after the outbreak of war, 100 seriously wounded soldiers were treated in them. By 1915 this number had increased to 3,000 patients treated and 300 operations successfully carried out. There were also seventeen hospitals for recovering wounded. Often these were in wings of large private houses. A large hospital for war wounded was opened in Plymouth in 1915. Over the course of the war hundreds of Devon women took up nursing war casualties. A Red Cross Hospital opened in Torquay in 1914.

There were eventually dozens of hospitals, large and small, around Devon performing tasks such as emergency surgery, smaller surgery and rehabilitation for those who had lost limbs or sight or whose serious wounds took longer to heal. Oldway Mansion in Paignton, once home to sewing machine manufacturer Singer, became a military hospital. To begin with the casualties were mainly British. In 1917, when the USA entered the war, many of their casualties were treated at Oldway. Recovering Americans out and about in Paignton caused quite a stir with their strange accents. They were often followed by groups of little boys keen to hear about the war and what it was like in America. Other large private houses that became military hospitals in Devon included the home of Mrs H. Barton at Budleigh Salterton, where she also worked as a VAD.

Devon Women Serving Abroad

Among these brave women were Phyllis Maltby, who served as a VAD in Malta. She was inspired by her father's military service in India. Sadly, she died at a young age from an illness directly related to her war work. Women often volunteered as ambulance drivers near battle fronts. Exeter nurse Elsie Knocker and her friend Mairi Chisholm began their service abroad as motorcycle dispatch riders. Unusually for the times, Elsie had been keen on motorbikes from a young age, which many people thought was shocking. Their time as ambulance drivers for a British doctor was unofficial and unpaid. Often when the fighting came close they were at risk of bombs and gas attack. Despite their unofficial status, help with equipment and medicines seems to have come through official channels.

Plymouth-born Nurse Olive Bennett served as a VAD nurse and died on active service in 1916. Her death was listed as a result of overwork in terrible conditions. She could easily have picked up an infection while nursing soldiers with gangrene or while dealing with infected amputated limbs. There were no antibiotic medicines at the time. Olive was missed off the list of war casualties and this was only rectified in 2017.

Women in Agriculture

As well as tasks such as moss collecting, young women without children increasingly became involved in agricultural work, usually instructed by experienced men who were either too old to join up or whose occupations were considered reserved. At first the women were viewed with suspicion by male agricultural workers. Would they be strong enough? Did they have enough stamina? Would they cope with the inevitable dirt, wet and cold? The answer to this was a resounding 'Yes!' Soon women were successfully involved in all aspects of farming. From planting to reaping, from forestry to ploughing, from looking after and using horses to dry stone walling, Devon's women were a success. Sadly, at the end of the war young women who wanted to remain in agricultural work were usually replaced by returning men, and this was also the case in many other occupations.

Soldiers' Letters

Often upbeat and hiding the awful truth about their war service (or heavily censored otherwise), soldiers' letters to loved ones are a testimony to their bravery and sacrifice.

A corporal from Barnstaple wrote that he had come out of the trenches having faced heavy artillery fire for three days. He wrote that he and his friends had been dodging snipers and had suffered heavy losses. However, he was uninjured and enjoying some relaxing fishing behind the lines.

A private from Barnstaple wrote that he had been injured, but not seriously and wanted to get back into the fighting. In spite of the enemy's shells and bullets and hand-to-hand fighting, he and his comrades had a job to do.

A sergeant from Holsworthy who had been invalided home spoke cheerfully to a reporter. He had been hit in the upper body by shell fragments, one of which had entered his neck and severely damaged it. Doctors had told him to expect problems in the future because of his injuries, but he was thankful to be out of the fighting. He had been rescued by brave stretcher bearers.

A doctor from Devon had joined a Devon regiment at the start of the war. He described life aboard a hospital ship. This account was given after the war and gives a realistic view of the terrible conditions. On his arrival, 500 wounded soldiers and sailors, some in a serious condition, lay on dirty blankets in every available space:

> I was alone to deal with this. I got men with slighter wounds to find cloth and tear it up for bandages. Thankfully someone found several bottles of turps, which I used to clean wounds and stop them bleeding. I had to make tourniquets from chair legs and rope, which I also treated with turps. After three days three medical orderlies arrived and I thanked God. I had only had brief snatches of sleep in seventy-two hours.

First World War Victoria Cross Recipients from Devon or in the Devonshire Regiment

Lieutenant Sir John George Smyth. Born in Teignmouth. Won the VC in 1915.
Colour Sergeant Alfred Joseph Richards. Born in Plymouth. Won the VC in 1915.
Private Theodore W.H. Veale, Devonshire Regiment. Born in Dartmouth. Won the VC in 1916.
Private Thomas Henry Sage. Born in Tiverton. Won the VC in 1917.
Second Lieutenant John James Crowe. Born in Devonport. Won the VC in 1918.
Brigadier General George Grogan. Born in Devonport. Won the VC in 1918.
Lieutenant Commander Arthur Leyland Harrison. Born in Torquay. Won the VC in 1918.
Lieutenant Commander Richard Douglas Sandford. Born in Exeter. Won the VC in 1918.
Lance Corporal George Onions. Won the VC in 1918.
Captain Theodore Bailey Hardy. Born in Exeter. Won the VC in 1918. A vicar, he was in his 50s when he joined up as an army chaplain. Many times he rescued injured soldiers both during and after battles. He was killed while attempting a rescue.

'Enemies' in Devon

In late 1914 the people of Plymouth were shocked when a ship with over 600 German and Turkish prisoners of war tied up at the docks. The prisoners were hastily herded into trucks and driven off to a secret location. A journalist at the time noted that they were mostly sailors with a few soldiers mixed in.

After escaping from a prison in South Wales, two German army officers were captured in north Devon. They were sent to a different prison camp.

At the start of the war, the Abbot of Buckfastleigh and several German monks were taken away for questioning. They were later allowed to return to the abbey.

When the war began a few Germans were living near Seaton and working as waiters and handymen in the town's hotels. Then a rumour began – the Germans were spies! Shortly after, army officials appeared in the town and the Germans were arrested and never seen again. At first the town was alive with gossip. Enquiries from hotel owners about their missing staff and what to do with their belongings were met with silence from officials. After several weeks the Germans became old news and their clothes and other items were given to the needy.

A Danish man living in Devon was taken prisoner after being found in possession of equipment suitable for sending telegraphic messages overseas. Denmark was a neutral country and the man was imprisoned as he was unable to give an adequate explanation for his activities.

A young Irish man travelled from his home country to Exeter with the hope of enlisting in a Devon regiment like his older cousin. Unfortunately, while trying to ask the way to the nearest recruitment centre his heavy accent was mistaken for German. This caused quite a panic and the man was jostled and then searched for weapons by members of the public. He was then arrested but set free. The arresting officer had family in Ireland himself.

DEVON FATALITIES

Sadly, every parish in Devon lost men in the war and carefully attended war memorials can still be seen today, often dedicated soon after the Armistice. The village of Copplestone, though, has a new one. This is not because the locals at the time didn't care about war casualties – far from it. Old boundaries meant that some Copplestone war heroes were commemorated on the memorials in other villages. Then boundaries changed. Today the names of Copplestone's nine First World War and one Second World War dead are shown on a memorial in the centre of the village. It was unveiled on 11 November 2018, 100 years after the end of the First World War. Parish councillor Stuart Penny, himself a former Army captain, gave the commemoration speech, followed by two minutes' silence at the village church. The memorial is made of local rugged stone left in its natural state, representing the area's land and those who worked on it.

Civilian Life in the First World War

At Exeter, Plymouth and other locations thousands of soldiers' children enjoyed Christmas parties in each year of the war. Each location had a large decorated Christmas tree and every child was supplied with a present, cakes and other treats. A number of Father Christmases were seen around Devon each December, leading to speculation about which was the real one!

Munitions in Devon

Though primarily an agricultural county up to the war, there was some industry and where possible such factories were converted so that they could take on war work. Shells, munitions, aircraft components, parts for military vehicles and guns, gas masks and uniforms were all made in Devon.

The End

On the eleventh hour of the eleventh day of the eleventh month of 1918, the war ended. This immediately led to the abdication of Kaiser Wilhelm II, who went to the Netherlands. Other Axis leaders also gave up their rule. This was a condition of the peace settlement as the allies wanted to rid Europe of the leaders who were seen to have led their countries into the terrible conflict. Thus ended 'the war to end wars'. If only …

18

BETWEEN THE WARS: SPANISH FLU AND VOTES FOR WOMEN

EDWARD VIII (1936)

At first glance Edward VIII was what the country needed after the horrors of the First World War. He was fun-loving and modern, and seemed to care about the country's poor. He was also a womaniser who had numerous affairs with married upper-class women who were not going to spill the beans and risk their reputations. Then it all changed. He fell in love with American socialite Wallis Simpson, who was married to her second husband, Ernest. She divorced him and married the King. He was forced to give up the throne as the church would not accept a divorced Queen Consort, particularly as she was twice divorced!

THE SPANISH FLU EPIDEMIC

In 1917 an epidemic of flu occurred. Most people who got it experienced the usual sore throat and aches and pains, but soon recovered. Then in 1918, just as the First World War was coming to an end, a deadly strain of flu broke out that swept the planet. It killed an estimated 50 million people around the world, including at least 250,000 in Britain and many hundreds in Devon. Early cases of Spanish flu occurred in soldiers in Étaples, France. There are various theories about the origins of Spanish flu but it is likely that it mutated from a form of bird flu. Severe symptoms were at first like those of pneumonia. Then lung tissue and other organs began to break up, leading to many people dying from oxygen starvation. As the war was ending, Spanish flu came to Devon when American troops in transit back home developed the disease while stationed in Paignton. They were taken to Oldway Military Hospital, where the illness was at first diagnosed as pneumonia. Around sixty American soldiers died of flu and were buried with full military honours near the hospital along with over 100 who had died of wounds.

As the war was coming to an end and victory was in sight public morale was high. Military authorities at first managed to withhold news that high numbers of troops abroad had got the flu and that many, weakened by the bad conditions and war stress, were dying.

Most deaths from Spanish flu did not occur in elderly or infirm people. Victims who died were often previously very fit and aged between 20 and 40. Pregnant women were very susceptible and usually this resulted in the deaths of the mothers and unborn babies. A lot of Devon schools closed because so many teachers and children were ill.

No one really knows why the young were so at risk. Possibly older people had gained some immunity from exposure in a less virulent epidemic in 1889–92.

Unlike many illnesses, living in an isolated area did not protect people from getting flu. Lots of out-of-the-way Devon villages reported deaths and in some cases the whole village would be affected, though most would survive. Worldwide, people on islands many miles out to sea with no contact with other people also became victims.

- Although called Spanish flu it didn't originate there, but Spain was the first country in Europe to openly report it in newspapers. The leaders of most countries involved in the war were, at first, reluctant to say too much as they didn't want to affect morale. Spain, as a neutral country, had no such reservations.

- There were claims that Veno's cough mixture could cure Spanish flu after some people taking it recovered, but many people recovered without it! Veno's company quickly quashed the rumour. Another 'cure' was to put a tin of road tar under the sufferer's bed as it was believed that the strong smell would kill the flu. Today we know that tar can actually be carcinogenic!

Newspapers from 1918 were a strange mixture of our troops' triumphs, influenza and harvest festivals. By 1919 the Spanish flu petered out, but it was considered the most deadly pandemic in history. More people around the world died of it than had died of plague in earlier centuries.

Dame Georgiana Buller and Orthopaedics

Dame Georgiana Buller's medical pioneering did not end with the First World War: she founded an orthopaedic hospital for children in Exeter in the 1920s. Georgiana had severe problems with her spine after falling from a galloping horse and realised that treatment was unavailable for poorer people who could not afford to pay for it. Often disabled people spent most of their time at home as many people still felt that disability was somehow shameful. Georgiana changed all that. Her Princess Elizabeth

Orthopaedic Hospital opened in Devon in 1937 for both children and adults. This was followed by training centres – one at St Loyes, Exeter – where people with disabilities were taught skills such as making parts for machines and tailoring. Soon training centres were established in other parts of Britain, giving pride, independence and an income to disabled people. Georgiana was helped in her efforts by Minister for Labour Ernest Bevin, who had lived in Copplestone as a child and had become her friend.

Members of the Buller family still live at Downes House, a beautiful eighteenth-century building with large grounds.

In 1927, the Duke and Duchess of York made one of several visits to Exeter. On this occasion they opened an orthopaedic hospital. The Duchess became known for her interest in medical charities and institutions. The Duke, of course, later became King George VI after his brother, Edward, renounced the throne.

VOTES FOR WOMEN!

Women had been quietly campaigning for the vote since the 1840s. Gradually their fight became more public. Emmeline Pankhurst visited Exeter, Plymouth and Barnstaple in 1914, when British suffragettes agreed to stop pressing their cause during the First World War and many of them became active in war work instead. In her rousing Devon speeches, Mrs Pankhurst spoke of the evils of Germany's behaviour and praised the men and women of Devon who had become soldiers, sailors, nurses and war workers.

Many Devon women supported one of the two suffragette movements. The National Union of the Women's Suffrage Societies (NUWSS) tried to win the vote for women by peaceful campaigning means. Their president was Millicent Garrett Fawcett. The NUWSS had over 50,000 members. In contrast, Mrs Pankhurst's Women's Social and Political Union (WSPU) advocated a more militant stand with widespread damage to property to highlight their cause. The movement initially had 5,000 members, but numbers grew. Emmeline was held in Exeter Prison and, like many suffragists, was force fed when on hunger strike. This involved forcing tubes up the victim's nose and down into her stomach, whereupon food was poured in. It was an excruciatingly painful experience and many never fully recovered their health. When Emmeline became ill she was released as the government didn't want any hunger strikers to die and become a martyr to the cause. Once Emmeline and her fellow suffragists were well they were rearrested. This became known as the 'Cat and Mouse Act'. Unfortunately, among the people who had little sympathy with the suffrage movement was the Bishop of London. He visited Holloway Prison to see Devon suffragette Rachael Peace, who was ill due to force feeding, but he claimed she was fine.

Eleanor Acland, of Killerton, was a suffragette who was against militant acts and was horrified by normally peaceful, respectable women breaking windows, damaging paintings and knocking the hats off politicians. Like many suffragettes, she was well educated and was an author. Amy Montague, of Crediton, was among a large party of suffragettes who went to London several times to attend rallies highlighting their cause.

Working-class suffragette Annie Kenney from Oldham, Greater Manchester, worked in a cotton factory from the age of 12. She was a member of the WSPU and among the first working-class leaders of the organisation. To rally working-class support, Annie gave talks around the country including in Torquay.

In 1918, women in Britain were given the vote, but only those over the age of 30 who owned a house or were married to someone who did. Finally, in 1928 all women aged over 21 were given the vote, the same as men.

NANCY ASTOR

Nancy Astor was born in Virginia, USA, in 1879 and came from a colourful and controversial background. Her father, Chiswell Langhorne, was a wealthy railway builder who had fought for the Confederate army during the Civil War and had been a slave owner until the Confederates were defeated. Nancy moved to Britain in 1905 when she married the wealthy Viscount Waldorf Astor, who was MP for Plymouth Sutton until his father's death. He then entered the House of Lords in 1919. Nancy promptly campaigned for and took her husband's place as MP and was the first woman to enter the House of Commons. Many people were horrified that a woman had been allowed to become an MP and claimed that she had only won the seat because her husband had previously held it. In spite of the eventual rise of the Labour Party, which changed the face of British politics, Nancy steadfastly remained a Plymouth MP until she retired at the end of the Second World War. She and her husband worked tirelessly in Plymouth for several charities, looked after wounded First World War soldiers at their home, helped their families and widows and took a great interest in the education and welfare of poorer children. Nancy Astor died in 1964.

> Nancy Astor may have been the first female MP to enter the House of Commons, but the first woman elected as an MP was actually Constance Markievicz, an Irish Republican and Sinn Fein member. She did not take up her seat.

19

THE SECOND WORLD WAR: BOMBS, SHORTAGES AND SMILING THROUGH

George VI (1936–52)

George VI never expected to become King; that task should have been his playboy brother Edward's. George was a shy, nervous man with a terrible stammer. He hadn't wanted to be King either! He took the role from a sense of responsibility. In spite of his problems though, George was a success, proving to be a conscientious, fair and hard-working king who became very popular with the people of England and was supported wholeheartedly by his wife Queen Elizabeth, later the Queen Mother.

Bombing in Devon

Plymouth

Plymouth sustained the worst bombing of any town in Devon during the Second World War. The proximity of Devonport Dockyard was the problem as this was a strategic target. Plymouth also had a number of industrial developments that were targeted as being of vital importance to Britain's war effort. On 20 and 21 March 1941 the worst air raid killed over 300 people and almost completely decimated the city centre. Some 3,700 houses were destroyed and over 6,700 other buildings were damaged or destroyed.

Three hospitals and several clinics were badly damaged, meaning that patients had to be moved to other locations, making co-ordination difficult. Over twenty churches were damaged or destroyed, as were schools and many pubs and cinemas. Just a small example of the hardship and danger faced by the people during other raids on Plymouth include:

> August 1941 – Several huge raids with incendiary bombs causing serious fires around the city.
> 14 June 1943 – Large 1,000kg bombs dropped, causing terrible damage.
> November 1943 – A raid targeting homes made huge numbers of people homeless. The Home Guard was on hand to help. Most were men who were too old to join the services. Their enthusiasm was legendary, even if they didn't have any equipment or uniforms to start with! Most Home Guard personnel worked at their regular jobs during the day, then turned out for guard duty at night doing fire watching and coastal defence.

Public buildings destroyed include The Athenaeum, a museum and library dating back to the Georgian era and built in a style reflecting ancient Greek buildings. Rebuilt after the war, the new structure included a theatre and later incorporated a cinema. However, the modern building is nowhere near as interesting as its predecessor.

Charles Church at Charles Cross has parts that are over 300 years old. During a bombing raid in March 1941 it suffered serious damage and it was decided to leave the shell of the church standing as a memorial to those who died in Plymouth's air raids.

Various plans for rebuilding Plymouth were suggested, but many locals were disappointed with the rebuilt city. Today some of Plymouth's modern buildings seem out of place when compared with surviving older ones.

Newton Abbot

Newton Abbot is a small town and not one that would seem to be strategically important in times of war. So why did the Luftwaffe risk planes and airmen to bomb the town? The answer lies partly with its proximity to Plymouth, but mostly in the fact that Newton Abbot Railway station lies on the route from London stations to Plymouth naval dockyard and was vital for moving armaments, materials and military personnel. Newton Abbot suffered a number of air raids. The worst one took place on 20 August 1940. Its objective – damaging the railway line and putting it out of action – was achieved, and nearly thirty people were killed and around 100 badly hurt in spite of the brave efforts of the RAF. Often small towns and villages near larger ones were hit either because they happened to be close or in order to spread panic.

Newton Abbot Railway Station

EXMOUTH

Exmouth is a lovely peaceful seaside town and may well have remained undamaged in the Second World War but for its location on one side of the River Exe estuary. This was the geographical feature that German bomber pilots looked out for on their way to bomb Exeter. Unfortunately for Exmouth, its location made it easy to find, too. Exmouth suffered a number of raids, resulting in over fifty deaths.

TORQUAY

In March 1942 three ships that were moored across the harbour mouth to stop a potential seaborne invasion were sunk by German bombers. Torquay and the Torbay area were not particularly strategically important but were targeted by the Luftwaffe, leading to hundreds of deaths and injuries. In May 1944 when Torquay was bombed, the bombers had a 'legitimate' reason for doing so. By this date the town was playing host to vast numbers of young American servicemen who were preparing for the D-Day landings.

TEIGNMOUTH

Teignmouth was bombed many times with large loss of life. The town was not strategically important and the Germans expended a lot of time and money doing this. The reason for this has never been clear – perhaps it was the fact that it had been popular with visitors and thus the attacks damaged morale.

EXETER

People often ask why Exeter, a non-strategic town, was bombed in the Second World War. It seemingly all began because the RAF had bombed the medieval city of Lübeck in northern Germany, decimating the old town. The RAF had been aiming at the nearby port, which was strategic, but unfortunately, as the town was close to the port it suffered badly, too. Hitler, so the story goes, was incensed at the destruction of the beautiful city and ordered that five medieval British cities should suffer the same fate. These, in order, were Exeter, Bath, Norwich, York and Canterbury. The bombings became collectively known as the Baedeker Raids as Hitler used a German language guide book to choose the cities. The book was written by a man called Karl Baedeker.

Exeter suffered nineteen air raids between 1940 and 1942, with the earlier attacks often lone planes. Unfortunately they killed over 100 people. Residents were frightened, but some were mainly fed up of air raids disturbing their sleep! Barns and outbuildings outside the city soon became makeshift bedrooms. Exeter was not expected to suffer massive air raids; after all, it was not a military base and had few industries. People from other targeted areas who had family or friends in Exeter had begun to move there for safety.

On the night of 4 May 1942, Exeter suffered its Baedeker raid. The attack took over an hour and involved forty German bombers. In that time over 175 people were killed and nearly 600 were injured, many seriously. The emergency services worked tirelessly to rescue people, provide medical assistance, put out fires and keep communications going – often by bicycle!

The 307 Polish Night Fighter Squadron were among the heroes of the Exeter blitz. They managed to shoot down four German bombers, despite being heavily outnumbered. The centre of the city and Newtown were decimated. Over 1,500 houses were totally destroyed, with a further 3,000 very badly damaged. Many of the city's shops were also destroyed. The city hospital was hit by incendiary bombs, designed to start huge fires. Staff bravely dodged flames to evacuate patients. Emergency services and volunteers continued to work after the blitz to rescue people trapped beneath destroyed buildings. Many were left homeless and in the amazing wartime spirit were given shelter, food and clothes, often by complete strangers. Exeter's iconic and much-loved St Peter's Cathedral was targeted in an attempt to destroy morale, but thankfully it sustained comparatively little damage. Other famous buildings were not so lucky. Beautiful Georgian Bedford Circus was so badly damaged that it had to be pulled down. This fine pair of curved Georgian terraces facing each other with lovely gardens between once rivalled Bath's Royal Crescent. Deller's Café, the place to be seen in Exeter, had opened in the 1900s offering elegant dining and surroundings at reasonable prices. Sadly, it was badly burned during bombing. Sections of the High Street with buildings dating from the 1600s were demolished. The organist at St Lawrence's Church on the High Street bravely kept playing during the raids until the building was hit and completely destroyed. No trace of the musician was ever found. A plaque marks the site of the church.

These are just a few of the buildings lost. The rebuilding of Exeter took twenty years as it was just one of many towns and cities to have suffered in this way and materials were scarce. Exeter has regular exhibitions and talks about the Polish 307 Squadron.

In Devon and many other areas of the country, the authorities were keen to avoid panic and loss of morale among the people. Often newspaper reports would play down the seriousness of bomb damage by saying 'some bombs fell' on whatever town. In reality the place may well have been very badly damaged. Today, the internet, mobile phones with cameras, and other devices would make this deception impossible.

Dunkirk and Brixham

Many Brixham sailors, along with others from other seaside towns, volunteered to take their boats across the channel to Dunkirk to rescue allied servicemen in May and June 1940. Many volunteered because they had sons and even grandsons in the services and, being too old to fight themselves, wanted to do their bit. Some proud but very aged Devon men were disappointed at not being allowed to go. By the end of the evacuation over 300,000 troops had been saved and one elderly rescuer christened the event the Grandpas' Armada!

The evacuation of troops from Dunkirk included thousands of French soldiers and many were housed in Plymouth. It was expected that they would return to the fighting, but France surrendered.

Devonport Dockyard

Today, Devonport is one of the largest naval bases in the western world and one of the oldest! Its history goes back to the Spanish Armada, and a fully operational dockyard was up and running by the 1690s. Devonport town was built to house shipyard workers and their families. Devonport is still the home port of many RN vessels and is a major centre for refitting and maintenance. Sadly, shipbuilding stopped in the 1970s.

Devonport Dockyard was a refit and repair facility during the Second World War with a highly skilled workforce, but a number of Navy vessels that saw active service were also built there before or during the war. These included:

HMS *Exeter*, a cruiser built in 1929. In 1939, *Exeter* was involved in the famous Battle of the River Plate where the German cruiser *Graf Spee* was so badly damaged that her captain scuttled her. Badly damaged herself, *Exeter* returned to Devonport for a major refit. Sadly, during the Battle of the Java Sea she was wrecked by Japanese forces. More than fifty of her sailors were killed and over 160 more died in Japanese captivity.

HMS *Gloucester*, a cruiser built in 1937. *Gloucester* was deployed to the Far East before being moved to the Mediterranean, where she successfully attacked enemy vessels and later protected convoys. In 1941 she was sunk by enemy aircraft off the Island of Crete where fewer than 100 of her 807-strong crew were retrieved from the water alive.

HMS *Britomart*, a minesweeper built in 1938. *Britomart* swept mines in the North Sea and the Arctic and Atlantic Oceans, clearing the sea ahead of cargo vessels. In 1944, *Britomart* was assigned to clear mines from the English Channel in preparation for the Normandy landings in 1944. During this work she was sunk by RAF planes, who mistook her for an enemy vessel. Twenty sailors were killed.

Pre D-Day Disaster

Today the village of Slapton is a beautiful and peaceful place, but on 28 April 1944 it was anything but. Annoyed village residents were moved out of their homes and relocated inland by military authorities. It was obvious that something big was going to happen, but the military were tight-lipped and remained so for many years. Because Slapton Sands Beach was very similar to those in Normandy, it had been chosen as a practice site for the Normandy landings. This was referred to as Operation Tiger and involved thousands of American servicemen. They were hard to hide and soon the Germans realised that something was afoot at Slapton. Things began to go horribly wrong very quickly. First the Americans were accidently fired on by their own side. Then those on landing craft were attacked by German torpedo boats that were waiting out at sea. Shamefully, the German boats had been seen the previous evening by a coastguard, who reported their presence but the message wasn't passed on. Nearly 750 Americans died; most either drowned or were burned to death in the wreckage of their boats.

Eventually local residents were allowed to return and it was obvious that something big had happened, but any questions were met with stony-faced silence from the military authorities. Eventually the facts leaked out and military leaders used the excuse that they needed a practice site for the Normandy landings. Maybe so, but Operation Tiger should have been undertaken with far more care and concern for those taking part.

In another horrible twist of fate, survivors of the Slapton Sands tragedy were later forced to take part in the real Normandy landings in June 1944. A memorial to the Americans who died can be seen at Slapton near the beach. It is hard to miss it as it includes one of the Sherman tanks used in Operation Tiger, which was rescued from the sea in the 1980s and lovingly restored. On 28 April 2019, the seventy-fifth anniversary of the terrible Operation Tiger tragedy was commemorated by a special service.

Devon's Devoted Daughters

The Women's Land Army began in the First World War but was disbanded at the end of the conflict. During the Second World War many male farm workers joined the military, causing shortages of labour. Before the war Britain had relied on a lot of imported food, and supplies became uncertain due to the conflict. It was soon realised that Britain needed to grow more of its own food, so the Women's Land Army was reformed. Rural Devon had many 'land girls', as they were known, and they came from all walks of life. They fact that they were often requited to work up to fifty hours a week came as quite a shock to some.

The women's uniforms included practical hard-wearing coats and trousers in drab brown colours, green jumpers, overalls that were designed for men and never fitted properly, rubber boots and thick gloves. Most Land Army Girls were proud to wear the uniform but found it very itchy.

The women did almost all the jobs that men would do, including dairy work. Milking cows came as a shock to some well brought up young women, but most soon got the hang of it. Other jobs included looking after animals, picking produce, making cheese, driving farm vehicles, muck spreading, hedging, sowing and harvesting crops. Many women found themselves being trained to kill rats and other vermin; another job that took some getting used to!

Some Land Army Girls learned forestry skills such as tree felling and replanting and timber sawing. One Devon woman, a Mrs Atkins, recalled, 'I remember the blisters I had at the end of my first day sawing wood. The manager took pity on me and let me do lighter duties for a bit. But my hands eventually became hardened and I could saw all day if need be.'

At the start of the war many Devon farmers, particularly older men, were unhappy at having female workers. 'Tis all wrong,' one exclaimed to a visiting official. 'They's women an' I aint never seen no women so dirty an' smelly!' Most farmers soon got used to the idea though.

The isolation of a lot of Devon farms took some getting used to for girls who were used to town life. Often attending the nearest entertainment meant a long walk there and back, although some farmers obligingly gave their Land Girls lifts. These were usually by horse and cart – no point in wasting limited petrol stocks!

Pigeon Private

An Exeter homing pigeon named Mary was awarded a Dickin Medal in 1945 after her loyal and brave work carrying vital messages. Mary often found herself flying through bullets and bombs but kept on regardless. Other brave pigeons and different animal species around the country also won the award – a medal with a blue and green ribbon. The Dickin medal is seen as the animal version of the Victoria Cross!

20

MODERN DEVON: NEW TOWNS, FILMS AND FLOODS

ELIZABETH II (1952–)

The rebuilding of bombed areas of Devon took over twenty years to complete.

PRINCESSHAY, EXETER

As well as people's homes, the severe bombing of Exeter demolished many shops and businesses. It was decided that a new shopping area was needed in the centre near to the site of Bedford Circus. This would replace many missing shops and be a boost to morale. Princess Elizabeth unveiled a plaque at the site in 1949. Seen as a symbol of recovery, the new Princesshay was the first vehicle-free shopping precinct in the country. Its name honoured the princess, the 'hay' at the end being a Saxon term for an enclosure or meeting place. It was designed by urban architect Thomas Sharp and from the outset there were some critics. A post-war shortage of building materials meant that Princesshay had a lot of concrete that was not very attractive. Sadly, by 2000 it was past its best and demolition began in 2004.

The modern Princesshay Shopping Centre

The new larger Princesshay opened in 2007. A mix of metal and lots of glass, it is very modern and striking to look at. Many people like the new vibrant Princesshay, but others say it fits ill with what is left of the old city. Well, you can't win 'em all!

In 2008, Princesshay hit the news when a man with mental health issues tried to set off a home-made bomb there. Thankfully it didn't go off properly.

DIG THIS!

After old Princesshay was demolished, archaeologists began excavations as the area is in the historic centre of the city. Their extensive archaeological finds included over 150 coins from the Norman period, hundreds of pottery fragments, Roman tiles and lots and lots of clay smoking pipes.

PLYMOUTH CENTRE

Not everyone is happy with Drake Circus, Plymouth's newest shopping centre that opened in 2006, and it has actually won spoof awards for ugliness. It is claimed that the exterior looks like overlapping sheets of giant cardboard set at a slant! The remains of Charles Church, which are over 300 years old, stand slightly in front of Drake Circus, an eerie but calm reminder of Plymouth's wartime ordeal. Modern Plymouth is well served with shops, theatres, cinemas pubs and sports centres. However, like other bombed towns, many people claim that the rebuilt centre of Plymouth has lost its charm and character. Others think that its former atmospheric narrow streets inhibited traffic and growth, and that post-war building got rid of a lot of old slums. This gives rise to another opinion – that some of Plymouth's post-war buildings are becoming modern slums themselves. The debate goes on.

MORE VISITS TO DEVON BY QUEEN ELIZABETH II

In 1939 Princess Elizabeth visited Dartmouth Naval College with her father, King George VI. This was apparently the point when she realised that she really liked Prince Philip of Greece and Denmark, who was a cadet at the college. He had been given the job of showing her around. She was 13 and he was 18. They married in 1947. Since 1939 she has visited the county on numerous occasions, including:

1949 – Princess Elizabeth unveiled a plaque in Exeter to mark the beginning of the building of Princesshay shopping precinct.
1952 – The newly crowned Queen Elizabeth visited several places in Devon.
1956 – Queen Elizabeth and Prince Philip visited Exeter University, Barnstaple Shopping Centre and Eggesford, where the Prince planted a tree.
1998 – The Queen visited Torquay and Topsham, where she visited the sixteenth-century Bridge Inn. She apparently took some bottles of local beer home for Phillip!
2012 – The Queen visited Exeter as part of her Diamond Jubilee celebrations. She viewed the new Princesshay Shopping Centre, opened in 2007.
2015 – The Queen and Prince Philip visited the Wrigley chewing gum factory in Plymouth. There they learned all about the production of chewing gum!

2018 – Queen Elizabeth visited Devonport naval base for the decommissioning of HMS *Ocean*. The ship, an amphibious assault vessel, had been the fleet flagship of the Royal Navy.

Some Visits by Other Royals

1969 – Queen Elizabeth, the Queen Mother, visited Devon to open a new YMCA near Torquay.
1982 – Princess Margaret opened the Theatre Royal, Plymouth.
1983 – Princess Diana visited a children's nursery in Exeter as a break from official duties. In the 1980s, it is said that Diana also visited a boyfriend who had a home in Devon!
1986 – Prince Charles and Princess Diana visited Lympstone Royal Marines Commando Training Centre. The couple later visited Ilfracombe to see a surf lifesaving club.
1993 – Prince Charles, interested in conservation and all things rural, opened Dartmoor Visitor Centre.
2004 – Prince Charles visited Exeter to see 21 The Mint, which had been renovated. Once part of St Nicholas Priory, it had been converted into a town house in the Elizabethan era.
2018 – Princess Anne visited the Royal Albert Memorial Museum in Exeter to mark its 150th birthday. The museum is named after her great, great, great grandfather, Prince Albert. Princess Anne was particularly interested in the Seaton Down Hoard. Anne also visited Torbay to talk to disabled Navy veterans.
2019 – Prince Charles and Camilla, Duchess of Cornwall, visited Devon on a tour. They called in at Sidmouth, where the Prince's great, great, great grandmother, Queen Victoria, lived as a baby.

Devon's Newest 'Castle'

In the early twentieth century, eccentric businessman Julius Drewe began to build Castle Drogo above the Teign Gorge near Drewsteignton as a home for his family. Famous architect Edwin Lutyens designed the castle, which is built of mellow granite. Unfortunately, building work was held up by the First World War as labour was short because so many men had joined up. The structure was not completed until 1930. Sadly, Drewe died soon after. Anyone passing Castle Drogo could be forgiven for not realising that it was built in the twentieth century. Its design looks medieval and at first glance has even fooled historians. The National Trust took over Castle Drogo in 1974. Unfortunately, Drogo was built with some serious design faults that caused damp and major roof leaks, so it has been closed to visitors for several years and covered in scaffold and canvas. Renovations are due to be completed in 2020.

Old Village

Copplestone is a village in the centre of Devon. The oldest house dates from around 1600 and could be earlier. The Cross, the village pub, was built in 1800 and became a pub around 1825. On the main road through the village, Porch Cottage housed the local policeman in the 1800s. One wall still remains and is part of an agricultural machinery repair centre, where it is still possible to see the window bars of Copplestone's tiny prison! A new police house was built in 1925 but there is no police presence today. In fact, it would be hard to find a policeman in the nearby larger town of Crediton. Copplestone was a thriving village up to the Second World War, although there were just a few hundred residents. There was a coal merchants, a saddlers, livestock markets and a tailors.

By 2001 there were 804 villagers, while in 2011 there were 1,253. Today there are 1,800 residents and 660 houses. More new houses mean the population will rise still further. Facilities, though, are not keeping pace. All the old businesses and facilities mentioned above closed years ago. There are youth clubs and coffee mornings at the local church. There is one small general shop/post office, but sadly Copplestone's only pub closed several years ago, removing the heart of the village. The local garage and hairdressers also closed. A mill on the outskirts of the village does now house small businesses. While a new sports field has been developed, a long-awaited village hall is yet to be built because of a lack of funds. It's an old story and one experienced by many small, slightly out of the way rural communities. The demise of businesses and facilities in Copplestone came about with the advent of motorised transport, making the 14-mile journey to Exeter and elsewhere much easier. People began to travel to larger shops and small village businesses couldn't compete.

Changes for the better may well be afoot though. Former local councillor Stuart Penny has highlighted the fact that Copplestone Railway Station has been revamped and more parking will mean that the station becomes a parkway, which should revamp the village and may bring in extra business. Now things may have gone full circle. Will ease of transport and a rising population actually bring more facilities for Copplestone?

New Town

Cranbrook is just a few miles from Exeter and the first houses were built there in 2012. The town is served by a number of buses and is on the Waterloo to Exeter railway,

Houses at Cranbrook New Town

making access to the city easy. There are around 4,000 residents currently living in Cranbrook and plans are afoot for the town to get much larger. On the plus side it is cheaper to buy a home in Cranbrook than Exeter or other nearby areas and the town's houses are attractive and well laid out with lots of greenery and a nice play park. The town is also surrounded by attractive countryside and is a short drive from the beaches of Devon's south coast. Its new 'Education Campus' for children from 5 to 18 seems to be successful. Critics, though, say that the town has no soul and has not got enough shops or things for older children to do. It is claimed that facilities will grow with the town, but residents seem sceptical in the current economic climate. When asked, East Devon District Council was reluctant to give any information on Cranbrook or its future development.

Other places called Cranbrook include: Cranbrook in Queensland, Australia; Cranbrook in Kent, England; and Cranbrook Iron Age Hill fort, Devon.

DEVON UNIVERSITIES

PLYMOUTH MARJON UNIVERSITY

Marjon University (University of St Mark and St John) received university status just a few years ago. Founded in the 1840s as St Mark's College, mostly religious subjects and teacher training were taught initially. Today, Marjon's subject base is wide, as you would expect from a university. It is a small institution though with around 3,000 students.

University of Exeter

In a roundabout way Prince Albert had a hand in the formation of the University of Exeter. After Albert's death in 1861 the Royal Albert Memorial Museum was built, recognising his talents. The RAMM attracted other important intellectuals and became known for the quality of its courses, speakers and exhibits. The Royal Albert Memorial College grew from these and after several name changes and amalgamations became the University of Exeter in 1955.

University of Plymouth

The origins of the University of Plymouth go back to the 1860s with a navigation school. It later offered tuition in other technical fields usually relating to maritime subjects. Plymouth Polytechnic began in the 1970s. Devonport Dockyard took students on work experience, and some worked there as their first job after graduation. A much wider range of subjects was added and the polytechnic became a university in 1992 in line with others around the country. The Peninsula Medical School is part of the university. Today, the University of Plymouth has over 20,000 students.

Exeter Airport

Located at Clyst Honiton, Exeter Airport is handy for people living in most areas of Devon and handles around 800,000 passengers a year. That may seem small compared with Heathrow, which handles 200,000 people every day, but flying from tiny Exeter is more restful. You can fly from Exeter to dozens of British and European destinations, including London, Edinburgh, Manchester, Jersey, Greece, Paris, the Canary Islands, Paris and Spain. Exeter Airport began in an even smaller way in the 1930s when flying was very new and the preserve of the more adventurous among the wealthy. In the Second World War it became an important military airbase for the RAF and Polish Air Force in the defence of the county. The United States Army Air Force also used it as a base for D-Day.

Some Devon Businesses

Tourism

Tourism is big business in Devon, with visitors staying in hotels, bed and breakfasts, static caravans and chalets, touring caravans and tents. And why not? Devon is a beautiful county with two coasts – the north rugged and dramatic and the south gentler but steeped in history. Added to those are the lovely rolling countryside with its famously red soil and the drama of rugged Dartmoor and Exmoor with their very visible evidence of ancient habitation. Then there are museums, historic sites, adventure parks and wildlife centres aplenty. In addition, Devon's mild climate makes it a winner. No wonder around 6 million visitors visit the county each year, making tourism its biggest industry.

Devon cream teas are big in their own right wherever there are tourists in the summer. The teas are comprised of scones cut in half with clotted cream and jam with tea to drink. Simple, outsiders might think. Well, no, actually. For years a debate has raged about the right way to eat your cream tea. Devon aficionados insist that clotted cream should go on the scone first, then jam on top of it. Some other areas – notably Cornwall – do it the other way round. It is surprising how adamant the ensuing debate can be! In 2010, a campaign was started to have Devon cream teas given a Protected Designation of Origin, so that nowhere outside Devon could call their scone treats a 'Devon Cream Tea'. In 2011, Cornish pasties were given this status.

Her Majesty's Naval Base Devonport

Built on the orders of William of Orange (later King William III), Devonport is the biggest naval base in Western Europe today. It is located to the west of Plymouth by the Tamar Estuary. Devonport is vast. There are twenty-five ship berths and fourteen dry docks for repairs. It is also the refit facility for Navy nuclear submarines. With 4,000 people, the dockyard is the area's largest employer and supports many smaller businesses. After nearly 300 years and constructing around 300 ships, from early wooden vessels to steam ships to submarines, shipbuilding itself stopped at Devonport in the 1970s.

The Met Office

The Met Office relocated from Berkshire to Exeter in 2003. It is a world-leading organisation with the most up-to-date equipment and expertise. As well as predicting the weather, most importantly any oncoming extreme conditions, the Met Office conducts climate research including global warming, monitors air quality, and liaises with other met offices and weather centres around the world. Over 1,000 people work there, with jobs including meteorologists, climate change scientists and other science positions, computer specialists and engineers, weather desk advisors, business advisors, administrators, clerical workers and library personnel.

Devon's Stradivarius!

Few people in Devon have heard of Arthur Richardson unless they are violinists. He was born in 1882 and began his working life as a wood carver. Arthur moved to Crediton as a young man and began to indulge his passion for violins, violas and cellos by teaching himself to make them! He particularly admired those made by the famous Stradivarius in the early 1700s. Arthur used local spruce, though it was not always easy to get wood of good enough quality. Arthur became one of the best twentieth-century makers and had completed around 300 instruments by the time he died. Today they sell for £15,000 or more.

Floods, Storms and Fire

The Lynmouth Flood, August 1952

Devon's worst natural disaster in modern times took place at the pretty north Devon seaside town of Lynmouth on 15 August 1952. It was the school holidays and as usual Lynmouth was charming visitors. Unfortunately, it was raining. A lot! But holidaymakers in Britain are used to wet weather and are determined to have a good time. However, this was about to change , with a tragic outcome, leading to the deaths of thirty-four people. Excessive rain on already soaked high Exmoor began to pour into the Lyn River, which soon became a deluge worse than anyone could remember. Lynmouth, which is on the coast and lower than Exmoor, was flooded as the river broke its banks and the water kept coming. The force of the water moved huge boulders and tree trunks, which partly blocked the river and caused the water to rise still further. People reported seeing cars being dragged along by the force of the water as if they were toys. Hundreds of houses and other buildings were destroyed or badly damaged, leaving people homeless. It took a long time to restore Lynmouth to its former glory, but with the help of the emergency services and willing people from nearby towns, the locals did it. A memorial commemorating those who died can be seen in the village.

EXETER FLOOD, 1960

October 1960 in Devon was the wettest anyone could recall. Indeed, statistics produced later showed that five months of rain fell in just one month. On 27 October, the River Exe overflowed and flooded the St Thomas area of the city. Some parts were 6ft deep in water and 1,000 houses and businesses were deluged. People were trapped in their homes or places of work and the police and rescue services in boats worked flat out to rescue them, paying particular attention to the old and the sick. As in other times of trouble, people from other communities helped out with temporary accommodation and clothes. It was a very worrying time for all those affected by the flooding, but children, being children, enjoyed the boat rides. And several days off school.

Eventually, as the flooding subsided to just a few inches, children in wellington boots enjoyed cycling though the water, but for the grown-ups there was the worry of trying to put their homes back together.

Then, on 3 December in the same year, there was another cruel twist of fate when another flood in Exeter caused even more damage. Flood defences built later have so far been successful and work is now being carried out to improve them further.

EAST DEVON FLOOD, 1968

Flooding on 10 July affected many areas of east Devon, including Sidmouth, Colyton, Newton Poppleford and Honiton. Several people died in the flooding and thousands of homes were affected, with roads suddenly turned into waterways. As one Sidmouth resident remarked with wry humour, 'The place has begun to resemble Venice, but muddier!' Livestock and pets were lost and rivers became fearful torrents, washing away bridges and hampering the movement of rescue services. As the flood began to subside, the fire service spent many days pumping away water, and older school children were employed to help residents clear up their homes.

The River Sid at Sidmouth also turned into a torrent in 2012. Many of the town's roads were a foot deep in water but were passable with care. Planning for better flood defences for the town began in 2018. Like many other south coast towns, Sidmouth is suffering the effects of erosion to its high cliffs located to the east. In the 1980s, people walking along the cliffs could look to the west and see all the way along the promenade. Today the cliffs have eroded by several metres, obscuring the view. Worse still, owners of homes on top of the cliffs have begun to lose parts of their gardens. Warnings of the dangers of rock falls onto the beach are prominent.

Dawlish Rail Away Line!

Built as part of the South Devon Railway in 1846, the picturesque seafront railway line at Dawlish has captivated generations of visitors and locals. The line hugs the coast, almost along the edge of the sea. To build it, Brunel's workers had to bank up the ground with tons of stone blocks before the lines could be laid. Unfortunately, Brunel seems not to have considered the effect of wind and wave erosion! There have been landslides and storm damage to the Dawlish line almost since it was built. Repairs were not effective. In the early 2000s waves were regularly hitting the line. Then, on 4 February 2014, there was a violent storm. Waves bigger than anyone had seen before tore away a long section of the bank on which the lines rested, then tore away the rails themselves. The bizarre sight of railway lines suspended several feet in the air brought many curious onlookers. This was much to the annoyance of homeowners nearby, whose properties had also been damaged. Tons of shingle and larger sea rocks had to be moved before repair work could commence and it was weeks before the line could be reopened. This caused severe transport problems for many people. Brunel was a brilliant engineer, but he had his failures and some people have taken to blaming his 'silly' location of the railway for the problems at Dawlish. But the line has been there for over 150 years. A new sea wall will now help.

Elsewhere along Devon's coast, erosion has is getting worse. People with expensive clifftop homes have begun to lose their gardens and in some cases parts of their houses. A horrible, upsetting, but natural phenomenon.

FIRE!

The Royal Clarence Hotel in Exeter's Cathedral Close was built in the 1760s. In its early days the Clarence had several names. Then, in 1827, the Duchess of Clarence, attracted by the building's sumptuous interior and first-rate entertainment, stayed there and the name stuck! The Royal Clarence was the first building to be called a 'hotel' in England rather than the usual 'inn'. Over the years the Royal Clarence became one of Exeter's most iconic buildings. In the early hours of 28 October 2016,

The Royal Clarence Hotel, as it used to look

a devastating fire occurred at the Royal Clarence Hotel in Exeter. The fire possibly began in an adjacent building that was undergoing renovation. Hundreds of firefighters were involved in shifts to extinguish the fire, and this took several days. Sadly, many of the Royal Clarence's original features were destroyed, although historic items that were saved were planned to be incorporated into a new building on the site, which was to be as similar to the original as possible. The site has now been sold.

Devon on the Box

Basil!

Just about everyone has seen the award-winning comedy *Fawlty Towers* (shown in 1975 and 1979) about a rude, inept Torquay hotel owner played by John Cleese. However, not everyone knows that the show was based on a real Torquay hotelier! Cleese and the rest of the Monty Python team stayed there while filming sketches for their show. This time the hotelier chose the wrong people to be rude to. The result was the *Fawlty Towers* series.

Where There's Muck There's Laughs

If you imagine a London family who have become disillusioned with city life and decide to buy a market garden in Devon instead, you have the plot of the comedy *Down to Earth* (shown in 2000–05). The series was indeed filmed in Devon and was based on the family's misadventures because they hadn't done enough research. From agricultural mistakes, unwilling children and suspicious locals to money troubles, the family eventually began to make a go of things.

JAM ON IT

Jam and Jerusalem (shown in 2006–08) is a gentle, but sometimes naughty series about a women's guild in rural Devon. The friendships, rivalries and misadventures of the women are played out while doing battle with their wider, staid guild organisation. There are some very funny characters: Dawn French plays simple Rosie, Joanna Lumley is dotty Delilah and Jennifer Saunders is slightly snobby Caroline.

BURGH ISLAND AND CHRISTIE MYSTERIES

Burgh Island is an unusual place. At low tide it is possible to walk to it from Bigbury-on-Sea, at other times visitors without their own boat have to hop on to the famous sea tractor. Its high wheels can cope with the depth and it tows a wagon with large wheels so that passengers are kept high and dry. The Burgh Island Luxury Hotel built in the 1930s is in typical art deco style: all huge wonderfully shaped mirrors, stylish lighting, ornate glass roof, elegant dining rooms, bedrooms with original furnishings and strikingly coloured sofas. Unsurprisingly, the hotel has been used as a location for a number of films and TV dramas, most notably for adaptations of Agatha Christie novels, namely *And Then There Were None*, *Evil Under the Sun* and *Nemesis*. Christie lived in nearby Torquay for many years and is commemorated in the town.

A bust of Agatha Christie

DEVON AT THE FLICKS

ANGST REPRESSED!

Multi award-winning *The Remains of the Day* (filmed in 1993) was partly filmed at Powderham Castle. The repressed butler, Stevens, is played by Anthony Hopkins. He has secretly admired the housekeeper, Miss Kenton (played by Emma Thompson) for a long time. When she leaves to marry, Stevens realises he should have revealed his feelings for her. Years later she rejects him again. It is a poignant story of lost opportunity.

SENSE AND NONSENSE

A tale of eighteenth-century snobbery and social climbing, *Sense and Sensibility* (filmed in 1995) is a fascinating period piece set among a group of wealthy young men and the women who would like to become their wives. All's fair when husband hunting and there is a lot of backstabbing. Who is the prettiest young lady? Who will marry whom, and which young man has the most money? The adaptation of the Jane Austen novel starred Emma Thompson, Alan Rickman and Hugh Grant.

HORRIBLE HOUND

The Hound of the Baskervilles (several film versions) is set in an atmospheric area of Dartmoor. A hideous and fierce black dog has been preying on members of the wealthy Baskerville family. After many twists and turns, Sherlock Holmes discovers that the person responsible is now next in line to inherit the Baskerville fortune. The story was based on the legendary black devil dogs said to roam Dartmoor, their red eyes glinting in the moonlight.

SHADY LADY

Though not filmed in Devon, the musical *My Fair Lady* (1964) has connections with the county. Cockney flower seller Eliza Doolittle is taken in by Professor Henry Higgins after he has made a bet that with elocution and lessons in manners he can turn her into a lady. The film starred Rex Harrison and Audrey Hepburn. The story is based on the former mill worker wife of Devon vicar Sabine Baring Gould, who was educated by her husband.

21

A BACK TRACK: MINING, WOOL AND MODERN/ANCIENT TRADITIONS

The object of this book has been to explore Devon's history from era to era. But mining and the wool trade were important in the county for many eras, and the question was: where to put them? Spread throughout the book, the impact of their importance would have been lost. So here they are as a chapter in their own right!

TIN MINING

Devon mining was already an important industry before the Roman Conquest. In fact, ancient Britons did a roaring trade with the Romans, who could not get enough of their tin.

TIN MINING METHODS

From prehistory, 'streaming' was a method of extracting tin whereby miners retrieved small fragments of tin that had been washed into shallow rivers. By the medieval era thousands of miners were actually digging mines looking for tin-bearing rocks.

By the late 1600s, as technology advanced, mines became deeper and larger. The introduction of steam-powered drainage in the late eighteenth and early nineteenth centuries meant that shafts could be dug to thousands of feet, although the largest ones seem to have been in Cornwall. Air pumps meant better ventilation, so by the early nineteenth century most tin mining involved digging a shaft and then tunnelling. Shallow tin lodes were depleted by this time. This usually meant that the miners had to climb down ladders for hundreds, if not thousands, of feet. There were many people killed in falls, usually on the way back up after a gruelling shift. The invention of the 'man engine' – mechanised lifts – in the nineteenth century meant that miners were at least spared a strenuous climb.

Tin mining was a lucrative occupation but very dangerous. Many miners were killed in rock falls and floods. Few could follow the profession into old age as the work was so tough.

Tin Extraction and Smelting

To separate tin from the rock in which it was found, the ore was crushed and unwanted stones removed. In the eighteenth century boys were employed from a young age to look after machines crushing iron-bearing rocks. Other boys would work picking out bits of tin ore. Early tin miners smelted the ore in a fire pit. This was a slow and inexact process that led to impurities in the tin. The invention of proper smelting buildings with temperatures controlled by bellows allowed more and better quality tin to be produced at a faster rate.

Tin Mining Laws

There were separate tin-mining regions in Devon, each centred on a stannary town – Tavistock, Chagford, Ashburton and Plympton – which served as an administrative centre.

So lucrative was the tin-mining industry that by the medieval era miners were almost above the normal laws of the land. Only miners accused of murder or serious violence could be sent to civil courts.

From the fourteenth century Lydford Castle was used as a prison for tin miners who had broken stannary laws – those governing tin mining.

Miners who cheated by claiming that they had mined more tin than they actually had, or tried to pass off inferior tin as pure, could be punished by having to swallow hot tin! Any miner daring enough to try to pull off large-scale cheating could even be punished by execution without a proper trial. Lawyers had a long and arduous journey from elsewhere in Devon onto Dartmoor and sometimes arrived after executions had been carried out! This became known as Lydford Law.

A poem by William Browne illustrates this dreadful mismanagement. It begins:

> I oft have heard of Lydford Law,
> How in the morn they hang and draw,
> And sit in judgment after.

Crockern Tor on Dartmoor became known as Parliament Rock from the 1300s to the 1750s. Open-air stannary court proceedings took place there as the tor was in the centre of Devon's tin area. The court's roughly cut granite judge's chair and table can still be seen. Hundreds of miners and officials would gather there for meetings. There seems to be no record of what they did during the bad weather that Dartmoor is famous for!

Tin mining stopped being a viable business in Devon in the twentieth century.

Other Types of Mining

Copper mining was also very important and lucrative. Devon Great Consols mine yielded hundreds of thousands of tons of copper in the mid-nineteenth century, and a railway was built to transport it and other minerals from Dartmoor to Morwellam Quay. A community grew at the quay with homes for the workforce, a school and pubs. Today Morwellam is a spectacular 'living history' site charting the lives of Victorian families involved in mining.

Awful Arsenic and Monstrous Manganese

Arsenic and manganese mining in Devon flourished in the Victorian era when, sadly, no one understood how dangerous they could be. Arsenic, from crushed rocks, was used in the manufacture of pottery and glass from the Georgian era. Today it is understood that this is a hazardous substance and its industrial use and safety are carefully monitored. In the Georgian and Victorian eras, arsenic poisoning used to affect those working with it badly and often caused cancer. But it wasn't only people who worked with it who were at risk. In Victorian homes it killed pests and bizarrely, given that it did this, arsenic was also used in beauty products to give women the pale skin they often sought.

Manganese has been used in steel production since the Georgian era. It is also used as a rust preventer and in colouring glass. It is still used today, but manufacturers now understand that it is very detrimental to health. Manganese used to cause a terrible neurological disorder known as manganism, which destroyed a sufferer's bones.

Woollen Cloth Production and the Wool Trade

From the medieval era to the Georgian, woollen cloth production was a major source of revenue and employment in many areas of Devon. Before the Victorian era, competition from other countries and wars interrupting trade led to a near terminal slump.

Cloth Production

Sheep

Devon is an ideal region for raising sheep. Much of the county such as Dartmoor and Exmoor is on high ground, and sheep thrive there when other animals would not. Sadly for medieval peasants, the rise in popularity of Devon woollen cloth led to the enclosure of land that they had previously been allowed to use. This meant that landowners had even more land to raise even more sheep! As keeping sheep became such a money-spinner, other sorts of agriculture began to be neglected. Laws to stop people owning large flocks were not always successful given the vast areas of land that some farmers had for grazing!

'Finishing' the cloth was a big industry at Exe Island in Exeter, with water wheels providing power. A large majority of Exeter's workers were involved in the cloth industry.

Spinning and Weaving

Although the woollen cloth trade was so important to Devon's economy, much of it was carried out as a cottage industry, especially in the early days. The wives and children of small farmers and labourers were often involved in spinning and weaving to supplement the family's income.

Fullers

Fulling was not the nicest way to make a living but the wages were good. Fullers had to clean the cloth to remove any dirt and oil that infiltrated the wool. The fulling process thickened the cloth and made it hard wearing. Sometimes the wool was put into vats with water and pounded by weights to help the cleaning process. Sometimes fullers would pound the material with their own bare feet.

Just to make cleaning wool even less of a fun job, human urine was used in the cleansing process. The wool was washed with soap before it was sold. So, that's all right then!

Shearmen

Shearmen in this instance did not actually shear the sheep. Instead it was their job to trim the surface of newly made woollen cloth. This ensured uniformity. It was a skill that was harder than it sounds and required a lot of concentration. Experienced shearmen could work fast.

Drying

The finished cloth obviously had to be dried and was hung up on racks, known as tenters, in drying houses. This prevented the cloth from becoming misshapen.

To attach the wool to the racks, special hooks were used. These were known as 'tenter hooks' and it is said that this is the origin of the phrase 'to be on tenterhooks', meaning feeling anxious.

Guildhalls were meeting places where members discussed pay, conditions and whom to hire and fire. Skilled workers in each trade were members of their own guild, which were very powerful. From 1471, Exeter's wool workers' guildhall, known as Tucker's Hall, provided support, advice and business opportunities for its members.

The Wool Trade

A lot of Devon's woollen cloth found its way to the Netherlands, where it was particularly favoured by the wealthy merchants and the upper classes. It was also popular in Spain and Germany. Some Devon cloth found its way to far-flung parts of the world. In 1830, Exeter canal basin was built, allowing larger vessels to take on cargoes. Cloth was a major export from the city for many years.

Tariffs once applied to incoming goods are listed on a metal plaque in the Customs House, which is open to the public. Today some of the items seem strange: livestock, human hair, chimney pots and carriages complete with horses to name but a few!

Exeter's city centre is where the most powerful and wealthy of the city's wool merchants lived. Today it is still possible to see some of their fine houses on the High Street; they are mostly shops now or banks and other businesses. Before the Second World War, it would have been possible to see even more of these splendid buildings, but sadly many were lost in the bombing of 1942.

In 1844 the railway came to Exeter and, like many other places, its sea trade with other areas of Britain was affected. Foreign sea trade continued on a smaller scale until the late 1960s. Today, in summer the river is awash (if you'll pardon the pun!) with canoes, rowers and small Exe cruise boats.

Other towns that were particularly important in the wool trade include Crediton, Tiverton, Barnstaple and Tavistock. Each had its own class of merchants and large-scale farmers who became very wealthy.

Ancient Devon Going Strong

To round off this journey through the fascinating history of Devon, we've come a full circle to finish with some ancient customs that are still carried on today.

Ottery Saint Mary Tar Barrels

Forget tame firework displays on November 5th! Instead, try Ottery Saint Mary, where each Bonfire Night a curious and extreme custom, the Flaming Tar Barrels, has been played out. This has been going on since the seventeenth century with obvious links to the Gunpowder Plot. It has been claimed that the event actually has pagan roots and was probably intended to scare away evil spirits. It is certainly scary! Each pub in the town has its own flaming barrel, which is lit and carried on the shoulders of a local man, or nowadays, possibly a woman. Thousands of spectators fill the centre of town as shrieking barrel carriers dash along with huge flames and sparks emitting from their barrel. It is passed from one carrier to another until it disintegrates, upon which it is left to burn itself out in the street. The carriers are protected by wet sacking and flameproof gloves, and water is on hand just in case! Being chosen to carry a barrel is seen as an honour offered only to people born in Ottery Saint Mary or those who have lived in the town for many years.

Lammas Fair

In early July, visitors to Exeter can see a curious procession. The lord mayor, dressed in official regalia, is followed by other civic dignitaries. The mace sergeant carries a long pole decorated with flowers and ribbons. On the end of the pole is a large white glove. The procession heads to the guildhall, where the mayor stands on the balcony brandishing the strange pole while spectators watch from below. The ceremony has been going on for over 900 years and marked the start of harvest in the hope that it would be a good one. Originally the ceremony coincided with a large fair, which took place on Cathedral Green. Lammas, or Hlaf-mass to give the ceremony its probable original name, dates back even further to Pagan times. And the white glove? This dates back to King Edward III and is a symbol of his protection.

Hunting the Earl of 'Rone

Just to be clear, there is no evidence that Hugh O'Neill, the banished Earl of Tyrone, ever set foot in Devon in 1607! Even so, every May bank holiday weekend over four days at Coombe Martin, 'Hunting the Earl of 'Rone' takes place. A boy is chosen to be the earl and he is chased through woodland by 'soldiers', who eventually catch him. 'Rone is then led through the town accompanied by dancers, loud music and a hobby horse. At various points along the way 'Rone is shot and killed, only to be brought back to life by the hobby horse! There is a lot

The 'Earl of Rone' is captured again!

of drinking involved, but the ceremony never gets out of hand. On the last day, 'Rone is taken to the beach by his captors and 'drowned', this time not to be revived. The real Earl of Tyrone became an exile in Spain.

WASSAIL!

The cider celebration of wassailing may well have its roots in pagan times. 'Waeshal' was a traditional Saxon greeting. Wassailing takes place on twelfth night. Traditionally the men of a cider-growing community would pass a communal cider bowl around themselves – a lot of times! The apple trees would be blessed and cider poured on the roots to thank them for their previous crop. Raucous music would be played and sometimes a group of mummers (travelling actors) would arrive to give a performance and the wassail song would be sung by everyone. Today, the ceremony remains the same but women join in, as the author of this book can attest!

The Wassailing Song
(Mid-nineteenth century, or probably much older)

Here we come a wassailing,
Among the leaves so green,
Here we come a wandering,
So fair to be seen.

Chorus:

Love and joy come to you,
And to your wassail too,
And God bless you and send you a happy new year,
And God send you a happy new year.

Our wassailing cup is made,
Of the Rosemary tree,
And so is your beer,
Of the best barley.

Chorus

We are not daily beggars,
That beg from door to door,
But we are the neighbour's children,
Whom you have seen before.

Chorus

Call the butler of this house,
Pull on his golden ring,
Let him bring us out a glass,
And better we shall sing.

Chorus

We have got a little purse,
Of stretching leather skin,
We want some of your money,
To line it well within.

Chorus

God bless the master of this house,
Likewise the mistress too,
And all the little children,
That round the table go.

Chorus

Good master and good mistress,
While you sit by the fire,
Pray think of us poor children,
A wandering in the mire.

Chorus

CONCLUSION

From Devon's early times and the challenges people faced, to modern Devon with its own issues, from war to peace; from heroes to villains; from comedy to tragedy. I hope you have enjoyed reading about this remarkable and beautiful county in *The Little History of Devon* as much as I have enjoyed writing about it. Like the county itself, the task has been challenging, exciting, difficult to quantify, full of variety and very, very interesting!

BIBLIOGRAPHY

Allan, John, *An Introduction to the Roman Legionary Fortress at Exeter* (Exeter City Council, 2005)

Badman, T., Brunsden, D., et al, *The Official Guide to the Jurassic Coast* (Coastal Publishing, 2005)

Baring Gould, Sabine, *A Book of Dartmoor* (Methuen, 1900)

Baring Gould, Sabine, *A Book of the West Being an Introduction to Devon and Cornwall Vol. 1* (Methuen, 1900)

Baring Gould, Sabine, *Devonshire Characters and Strange Events* (John Lane Bodley Head, 1908)

Bayne-Powell, R., *Travellers in 18th Century England* (J. Murray, 1951)

Bidwell, Paul, T., *Roman Exeter: Fortress and Town* (Exeter Museum Service, 1980)

Birchall, James, *England Under the Tudors and Stuarts* (Home Library, 1927)

Cotton, R.W., *Barnstaple and the Northern Part of Devonshire During the Great Civil War* (Unwin Brothers, 1789)

Fox, A., *Prehistoric Hill Forts of Devon* (Devon Books, 1996)

Gant, T., *Discover Dartmoor* (Baron Jay, 1978)

Gaskell, Edward, *A History of Plymouth* (2001)

Greenhill, B. and Giffard, Anne, *The Merchant Sailing Ship: A Photographic History* (David and Charles, 1970)

Hart, Peter, *The Great War 1914–1918* (Profile Books, 2014)

Heine, H., *The Battle of Hastings* (1855)

Hoskins, W.G., *Devon* (Phillimore, 2003)

Hyman, N., *Sidmouth, A History* (Sidmouth Museum, 2016)

Isaac, W., *Cottage Scenes During the Cholera* (Coppard, 1848)

Lytton Strachey, Giles, *Queen Victoria* (Chatto and Windus, 1951)

Macfarlane, A., *Witchcraft in Tudor and Stuart England* (Routledge, 1999)

Marlow, J., *Kings and Queens of Britain* (Arctus Publishing, 1977)

Norway, A.H., *Highways and Byways in Devon and Cornwall* (Macmillan, 1911)
Page, W. (ed), *The Victorian History of the County of Devon* (James Street, 1906)
Pascoe, W.H., *Extraordinary Exmouth* (Obelisk Publications, 1991)
Parker, David, *Early Victorian Devon 1830–1860* (David Parker, 2017)
Pemberton, Clive, *The Origin and Story of Kents Cavern* (Algonquin Books, 1985)
Petit, P., *Prehistoric Dartmoor* (David and Charles, 1974)
Platt, Colin, *Medieval England, a Social History and Archaeology from the Conquest to AD 1600* (Routledge & Kegan Paul, 1978)
Plumb, J.H., *The First Four Georges* (Little, Brown and Company, 1975)
Quennell, C.H.B. and Quennell, M., *Life in Prehistoric Times* (Batsford Ltd, 1959)
Shapter, Thomas, *The History of Cholera in Exeter in 1832* (S.R. Publishers Ltd, 1971)
Stone, Avril, *The Book of Barnstaple Vol. 2* (Halsgrove Community History, 2003)
Tait, Derek, *Plymouth Through Time* (Amberley Publishing, 2010)
Wasley, G., *Devon at War 1939–1945* (Devon Books, 1995)
Weston, Agnes, *My Life Among the Blue Jackets* (James Nisbet & Co., 1913)
Whinray, James, *Devon Legends* (Tor Mark Press, 1996)
Wilson, Roger, J.A., *Roman Remains in Britain* (Constable, London, 1974)
Reports and Transactions of the Devonshire Association (1867, Vol. 2)
Reports and Transactions of the Devonshire Association (1871, Vol. 4)
Reports and Transactions of the Devonshire Association (1876, Vol. 7)
Reports and Transactions of the Devonshire Association (1883, Vol. 15)
Trewman's Exeter Flying Post (1914–1915)
The Western Times (1918)

INDEX